THE QUEEN'S LIFE

THE QUEEN'S LIFE

and Her Twenty-five Years of Monarchy

Graham and Heather Fisher

ROBERT HALE · LONDON

© Graham & Heather Fisher 1976

First published in Great Britain 1976

ISBN 0 7091 5773 8

Robert Hale Limited
Clerkenwell House
Clerkenwell Green
London ECIR OHT

Printed in Great Britain by Bristol Typesetting Co. Ltd,
Barton Manor, St. Philips, Bristol

Contents

	Authors' Foreword	9
	The Royal Web	13
1	The Queen's Life	17
2	Childhood	36
3	Royal Apprenticeship	44
4	Accession and Coronation	58
5	The Years of Monarchy	71
6	The Queen's Travels	97
7	Royal Consort	114
8	Heir to the Throne	129
9	The Queen's Homes	141
10	All The Queen's Men	153
11	The Cost	161
12	Can Monarchy Survive?	174

Appendices
I	The Queen's Diary	181
II	The Succession	185
III	The Queen's Travels	186
IV	Prince Philip's Travels	188
V	The Queen's Household	191
VI	The Cost	193
VII	Queens of England	194
	Index	195

Illustrations

facing page

The Princess, aged ten, with her family   32

Before going for a ride at Windsor on her thirteenth birthday   32

Learning to tie a knot as a Girl Guide   33

The Princess changes a wheel   33

Her last days as Princess. Nairobi, 1952   48

At work in Buckingham Palace   48

The Royal wedding of 1947   49

The new Queen in Edinburgh   96

The Queen's guests at a dinner party   96

The Queen's first Christmas broadcast, 1952   97

An old lady talks to the Queen. New Zealand, 1954   97

Time off on the farm at Balmoral   112

On a visit to Rothes Colliery, Kirkcaldy   112

Royalty and De Gaulle go to the ballet   113

The Queen, surrounded by Ghanaians, on the tour of 1961   113

The Queen in casual, weekend clothes   144

The Queen and Prince Philip pay silent tribute,
Aberfan 1966   144

A Derby to remember. The 1968 race   145

The Queen chatting to Princess Anne   145

The Queen with President Nyerere of Tanzania   160

The Queen and Prince Philip on a state visit to Mexico   161

The Queen and Emperor Hirohito in Japan, 1975   161

Authors' Foreword

In our earlier book, *The Crown And The Ring*, published to mark the Queen's silver wedding anniversary, it was perhaps natural that we should have focused more on her courtship and marriage than on her years of monarchy, more on personal life than public image.

This book, written to commemorate her Silver Jubilee on 6th February 1977, will perhaps redress the balance. It attempts a portrait of the Queen as a monarch. It attempts also a landscape covering the twenty-five years since she first flew back from Kenya on the death of her father—twenty-five years in which she has travelled the equivalent of something like sixteen times the circumference of the world, visited some fifty overseas countries as well as several hundred towns and cities in Britain, climbed skyscrapers and descended mines, planted trees and launched ships, opened schools and inspected hospitals, made around a thousand speeches and shaken hands with tens of thousands of people. She has also brought up four children.

Because she has also brought up four children, because she is wife and mother as well as Queen, because the twin images of woman and monarch overlap sometimes so closely that they are virtually indistinguishable, some aspects of her personal life inevitably come into the story.

In compiling this book, we have drawn upon our own recollections and research over the entire twenty-five years the Queen has been on the throne and we are indebted to all those who have helped us at one time or another. Their names are too numerous to list here and some would perhaps not wish to be listed. Nevertheless, they have our grateful thanks.

We are especially grateful to Mr Raymond J. Fullagar for his more recent research on our behalf and to Mrs Michael Wall,

C.V.O., Her Majesty's Assistant Press Officer, for her helpful answers to our many questions. The interpretation of Mr Fullagar's facts and Mrs Wall's answers is, of course, our own.

G. and H.F.

Keston Park,
Kent

**For
JOANNA
(when she is older)**

" A marriage . . . must be held firm in the web of family relationships between parents and children, grandparents and grandchildren, cousins, aunts and uncles."—The Queen, speaking on her silver wedding day.

THE ROYAL WEB

The Queen
Elizabeth Alexandra Mary, born 21st April 1926, married 20th November 1947, succeeded 6th February 1952, crowned 2nd June 1953.

Her Husband
Prince Philip, Duke of Edinburgh, born 10th June 1921.

Her Children
Charles, Prince of Wales, born 14th November 1948.
Princess Anne, born 15th August 1950.
Prince Andrew, born 19th February 1960.
Prince Edward, born 10th March 1964.

Her Son-in-Law
Capt. Mark Phillips, born 22nd September 1948, married Princess Anne 14th November 1973.

Her Father
King George VI, born 14th December 1895, succeeded 11th December 1936, died 6th February 1952.

Her Mother
Queen Elizabeth, the Queen Mother, born Lady Elizabeth Bowes-Lyon 4th August 1900, married the then Duke of York 26th April 1923.

Her Mother-in-Law
Princess Andrew of Greece, born Princess Alice of Battenberg 25th February 1885, died 5th December 1969.

Her Sister
Princess Margaret, born 21st August 1930.

Her Brother-in-Law
Earl of Snowdon, born Antony Armstrong-Jones 7th March 1930, married Princess Margaret 6th May 1960.

Her Sister's Children

David, Viscount Linley, born 3rd November 1961.

Lady Sarah Armstrong-Jones, born 1st May 1964.

Her Grandfather

King George V, born 3rd June 1865, succeeded 6th May 1910, died 20th January 1936.

Her Grandmother

Queen Mary, born 26th May 1867, died 24th March 1953.

Uncles and Aunts

Duke of Windsor, born 23rd June 1894, succeeded 20th January 1936, abdicated 11th December 1936, married Mrs Wallis Warfield 3rd June 1937, died 28th May 1972.

Mary, Princess Royal, born 25th April 1897, married sixth Earl of Harewood, died 28th March 1965.

Duke of Gloucester, born 31st March 1900, died 10th June 1974.

Princess Alice, Duchess of Gloucester, born 25th December 1901 Lady Alice Montagu-Douglas-Scott, married Duke of Gloucester 6th November 1935.

Duke of Kent, born 20th December 1902, killed on active service (in an air crash) 25th August 1942.

Princess Marina, Duchess of Kent, born 1906 Princess of Greece and Denmark, married Duke of Kent 29th November 1934, died 27th August 1968.

Cousins

Prince William of Gloucester, born 18th December 1941, died (in air crash) 28th August 1972.

Richard, Duke of Gloucester, born 26th August 1944, married Birgitte van Deurs 8th July 1972.

Edward, Duke of Kent, born 9th October 1935, married Katharine Worsley 8th June 1961.

Princess Alexandra, born 25th December 1936, married Hon. Angus Ogilvy 24th April 1963.

Prince Michael of Kent, born 4th July 1942.

Earl of Harewood, born 7th February 1923.

Gerald Lascelles, born 21st August 1924.

Her Cousins' Children

Gloucester: Alexander, Earl of Ulster, born 24th November 1974.

Kents: Earl of St Andrews, born 26th June 1962.

Lady Helen Windsor, born 28th April 1964.

Lord Nicholas Windsor, born 25th July 1970.

Ogilvy : James, born 29th February 1964.
    Marina, born 31st July 1966.
Harewood : David, Viscount Lascelles, born 21st Octo-
    ber 1950.
    James, born 5th October 1953.
    Robert, born 14th February 1955.
    Mark, born 5th July 1964.
Lascelles : Henry, born 19th May 1953.
Her Sisters-in-Law
Princess Margarita of Hohenlohe-Langenburg, born 18th
    April 1905.
Princess Sophie of Hanover, born 26th June 1914.
Princess Theodora of Baden, born 30th May 1906, died
    16th October 1969.
Their Children
Margarita : Prince Kraft, born 1935.
    Prince George, born 1938.
    Prince Ruprecht and Prince Albrecht
        (twins), born 1944.
    Princess Beatrice, born 1936.
Theodora : Prince Maximillan, born 1933.
    Prince Ludwig, born 1937.
    Princess Margarita, born 1932.
Sophie (first marriage) : Princess Christina, born 1933.
    Princess Dorothea, born 1934.
    Prince Karl, born 1937.
    Prince Rainier, born 1939.
    Princess Clarissa, born 1944.
(second marriage) : Prince Guelf, born 1947.
    Prince George, born 1949.
    Princess Frederika, born 1954.
Prince Philip's Uncle
Earl Mountbatten of Burma, born 25th June 1900.
Philip's Cousins
Lady Patricia Mountbatten, born 14th February 1924,
    married seventh Baron Brabourne 26th October 1946.
Lady Pamela Mountbatten, born 19th April 1929, mar-
    ried David Hicks 13th January 1960.
Their Children
Patricia : Norton, born 1947.
    Michael, born 1950.
    Joanna, born 1955.
    Amanda, born 1957.

Philip, born 1961.
Nicholas and Timothy (twins), born 1964.
Pamela: Edwina, born 1961.
Ashley, born 1963.
India, born 1967.

I

The Queen's Life

On that February day in 1952 when her father died and the young Princess Elizabeth found herself unexpectedly Queen, a message from London was received over the single telephone line which linked the isolated lodge at which she was staying in Kenya with the outside world.

For the purpose of completing the Declaration of Accession it was necessary to know what name the new Queen proposed to take.

The question was understandable (though perhaps not, at that time, to the Queen). Monarchs have not always ascended the throne in their given names. The Queen's own father, in fact, whose first name was Albert, selected the last of his four names, George, for the purposes of future monarchy. By doing so, by perpetuating his father's name, he hoped to paper over any cracks caused by his brother's abdication.

It was little more than an hour since the Queen had first learned of her father's death. In the privacy of her bedroom she had been crying and her face was still pale and strained as she sat at her desk in the stone and cedar sitting-room of the lodge. But her reply was unhesitating and definite.

" My own, of course—what else?"

So Her Royal Highness Elizabeth Alexandra Mary, Duchess of Edinburgh, became Queen Elizabeth II, sixty-second monarch—but only the seventh Queen in her own right*—to occupy the throne since the days of Egbert of Wessex, the first king of all England.

It was a role towards which she had been carefully coached

* Appendix VII.

B

and disciplined from the age of ten, when the abdication of her
Uncle David and the accession of her father made her next in
the line of succession. Much of the coaching came from her
father who, on his own admission, had "never even seen a state
paper" when he unexpectedly found himself king and was
firmly determined that his daughter should be better equipped
when her time came. The disciplining came from her paternal
grandmother, Queen Mary.

Queen Mary was a Royal of the old school. With her, royal
duty came first. Before private desire or personal heartbreak.
Before anything and everything. When her eldest son abdicated
to become the Duke of Windsor, she never forgave him and
would never consent to meet the American divorcee for whom
he gave up the throne.

It was this rigidly dutiful woman who for fifteen years, and
perhaps even before that, painstakingly drilled her grand-
daughter on the barrack square of royal discipline and in 1952,
when the Queen succeeded to the throne at the youthful age
of twenty-five, those years of youthful discipline were to stand
her in good stead.

There was, at the outset, much about her which reminded
many of those around her of Queen Mary. The same dignity
and composure, the same tight control over her emotions, the
same sense of duty. Over the years since, she has perhaps un-
bent in public in a way Queen Mary would never have done,
but only occasionally and only slightly.

But if some of those around her saw her as cast in the same
dutifully regal mould as her grandmother, it was her father that
she herself took as her principal model.

With the move from Clarence House to Buckingham Palace,
she took over her father's gilt-handled Chippendale desk at
which she still works today. Framed photographs of him watched
her from a side table as she worked at the desk, as they do
still today.

"Did my father do it?" she inquired when some point concerning coronation procedure was put to her. Told that he had,
she said, "Then I will, too."

She told Maurice Watts, who had been her father's page and
was now her page, "I want everything to continue exactly as
it did under my father."

Watts took her at her word. At Clarence House, in the relatively free-and-easy days when the Queen was still Duchess of Edinburgh, it had been the practice for any of her aides who wished to see her simply to tap on the door of her sitting room and walk straight in. It was a practice which was quickly discontinued following the move to Buckingham Palace.

The first royal aide who attempted to perpetuate the old tap-and-walk-in routine found himself deftly intercepted by the Queen's page. All future visitors to Her Majesty, whoever they were, must be properly announced, he was informed.

And the Queen herself soon made it equally clear that neither her youth nor her inexperience constituted grounds for any diminution of majesty. Those who may have thought that they had only a slip of a girl to deal with, like the courtier who relaxed against the mantelpiece while talking to her, were speedily disillusioned. " Are you feeling unwell?" the Queen inquired quietly. But the question was accompanied by a look of such displeasure that the courtier sprang to attention with all the alacrity of a guardsman on parade.

Neither then nor later did the Queen show any evidence of her father's famous temper. There was no need. She has an infinitely better weapon in her feminine armoury, a look (say those who have experienced it) which can almost kill at twenty paces. She employed it once at a dinner party to halt her husband in mid-sentence. She used it with equally telling effect on another occasion on Australia's John Gorton.

The Australian Prime Minister was among those who picnicked with the Royals on the Great Barrier Reef one day in 1970. The picnic quickly developed into a highly informal occasion with everyone ducking everyone else in the sea. Even Prince Philip and daughter Anne came in for the treatment, and John Gorton saw no reason for the Queen to stay dry. " Then I looked at her and there was something about the way she looked back," he has said.

With her accession to the throne, the Queen's life, like the lives of her father and grandfather before her, became increasingly dominated by the calendar and the clock. Year after year since, the same things have come round with almost clockwork regularity. In a sense, the Queen's life has almost the same built-in monotony as that of a car-worker on a production line and some people would find it just as boring. The Queen does not.

The pattern starts afresh each year with the publication of her New Year's Honours List and ends, to all intents and purposes, with her telecast the following Christmas. In between come such time-honoured hardy annuals as the Birthday Parade (which she has continued to hold in June, as her father did, though her birthday is actually in April), the Royal Maundy, the annual service of the Knights of the Garter in St George's Chapel, Royal Ascot, the Cenotaph on Remembrance Day and the opening of Parliament, along with Privy Councils and investitures, garden parties, receptions and banquets, hospital openings and factory inspections, bouquets and speeches, smiles and handshakes, six weeks at Windsor, weekends at Sandringham, the long summer stay at Balmoral.

The Queen's father was once described as " one of the very few men in the world who never gets a complete holiday." What was true of him is equally true of his daughter. So what about those two months at Balmoral each summer? Is that not a holiday? We quote what the Queen's former Private Secretary* told a Parliamentary Select Committee in 1971 :

" Every day of the year, wherever she is, the Queen receives from her ministers at home and her representatives in the rest of the Commonwealth and in foreign countries, information in the form of telegrams, despatches, letters. Her mail averages 120 letters a day. Thus she can never enjoy a complete holiday. Always at the end of the day there are papers to read and sign."

And sometimes at the beginning of the day, too. At Balmoral, on holiday, the Queen will frequently come down for breakfast in her riding gear only to find that there are letters to be read and documents to be dealt with, perhaps an hour or more's work to be got through, before she is actually free to go riding.

Another example. The day before her youngest child, Prince Edward, was born, the Queen worked at her desk as usual. And the day following his birth she had her dispatch box brought to her bedroom so that she could go through its contents while sitting up in bed.

" Nobody who does not carry such a burden is in a position to appreciate the strain it imposes," Adeane told the Select Com-

* Now Lord Adeane.

mittee. " The Queen is never free to do as she likes in the way that ordinary men and women are or to take a complete holiday. Her job is continuous and she cannot, like other hard-worked people, look forward to a period of retirement at the end of it."

One gathers from all that that the Queen is as dutiful as even Queen Mary could have wished. But what is she like—*really like*—in other respects? The honest answer is that no one really knows. No one, that is, outside the immediate family circle of her husband, children and mother . . . and they are not telling.

One knows, of course, what she is like physically. Her hair, blonde in childhood, is (perhaps with a little help from her hairdresser) a warm brown these days. Her complexion is good and her carriage upright. Her eyes have been described as " sea blue ". If that is meant to convey that they can change, as the sea does, according to mood, then the description is perhaps apt. In the privacy of her palace home, when she removes her shoes and plods around barefooted to relieve aching leg muscles, she is smaller than she appears in public. Her actual height is 5 feet 4 inches.

It is known that she likes dogs and horses, enjoys riding and loves going to the races. All else is an enigma. But it is possible, from fragments of information acquired piecemeal over the years, to attempt at least a partial portrait.

In a sense, it would seem that there are two Elizabeths. There is Her Most Excellent Majesty Queen Elizabeth the Second, by the Grace of God Queen of the United Kingdom of Great Britain and Northern Ireland and of Her other realms and territories, Head of the Commonwealth, Defender of the Faith, Sovereign of the British Orders of Knighthood and so on and so forth. This is the only Elizabeth most people know.

But behind Her Most Excellent Majesty lurks another Elizabeth : Elizabeth Windsor, woman, wife and mother, who will toss her head back and laugh uproariously when something amuses her, who has been known to let out a scream in the middle of a horror film, a wild whoop in the excitement of a Scottish reel and a yell of encouragement to her jockey during a close-fought finish at the races.

Sometimes only a matter of minutes separates one Elizabeth from the other.

The Queen was on one of the many overseas tours she has

carried out during her years of monarchy. Which and when does not matter, for the same thing (or something very like it) has happened many times. She returned to her coach on the royal train after a whistle stop at some small wayside halt, nudged off her shoes, wiggled her toes and sat with her feet up to rest her aching legs. The Queen was temporarily off-duty and the woman behind the Queen took over briefly, her face animated as she chatted with members of her retinue. Someone said something amusing. Back went her head and out came her laugh. " Full-blooded—right from the heart," friends say of the Queen's laughter. Then a warning blast on the train's whistle heralded the approach of another stopping place. Instantly her laughter ceased. On went her shoes, on went her hat and on went the impassive royal mask she wears so often in public.

Two things perhaps share responsibility for her public impassiveness. One is the inherited shyness handed down from her father. The other is her disciplinarian grandmother's long years of training. Even after more than thirty years of public life (if you include the engagements she carried out while still a Princess), the Queen has never completely conquered her shyness. She still finds it difficult to make small talk with strangers and the so-called " walkabouts " which have been a feature of royal visits since 1970 sometimes make her feel tense. A close observer who saw her at a film première not long back was surprised by the degree of tension she exhibited as she moved slowly along the line-up of waiting movie stars. " Her hands were so tightly clenched I thought her gloves would split at any moment."

But the self-discipline drilled into her by Queen Mary can work both ways. " I have been trained never to show my feelings in public," the Queen herself said once, and she more than proved it the time a New Zealand bishop, flustered by the pomp and ceremony of the occasion, welcomed her to his cathedral with a curtsy instead of a bow. While some of those with the Queen could not quite suppress a smile, not by so much as the twitch of an eyebrow did she herself betray whatever amusement she may have felt.

But, on balance, shyness and self-discipline have combined to create the legend of a largely unsmiling Queen. " Please smile more, Your Majesty," the mass-selling *Bild Zeitung* urged when she toured Germany. " Are you sure you're smiling enough ?" the

Queen Mother was moved to inquire over the telephone on one occasion when her daughter was in Canada.

But the woman behind the Queen, once she is away from the public limelight, invariably sees the funny side of things. Sometimes, as the film *Royal Family* fleetingly revealed, she will regale her family with her own witty account of a particular incident. She has even been known, in the privacy of the family circle, to turn amateur comedienne and act out the events of her public day.

She is, in private, a not inconsiderable mimic with a whole range of accents at her disposal. There was, for instance, the occasion when, bound for a public function, she felt a spot of rain just as she was getting into her car. " It's bloomin' rainin' and I ain't got me brolly," she said in accents which would have done credit to Eliza Doolittle.

Outside her family, few people have ever heard the Queen crack a joke. She is quite content to leave public wisecracking to her more extrovert husband and, these days, to her eldest son (who would seem to be witty enough for the whole family). We can think of only one occasion when she has permitted something approaching a joke to creep into a public speech. It was at the celebration lunch to mark her silver wedding anniversary.

" I think everyone will concede," she said, smiling, " that on this of all days I should begin my speech with the words, ' My husband and I '."

Witty asides may be more frequent, though, again, we can think of only one. " The perfect place for an assignation," the Queen murmured as she was guided through the shadowy surrounds of the nocturnal mammal house at London Zoo.

Not, of course, that anyone would want the Queen to play the comedienne on public occasions. Yet the fact remains that she appears most human on those rare occasions when her shyness vanishes, childhood training is forgotten and the real woman shows through. There was such an occasion when she opened Parliament in her first year of monarchy. In the words of an American artist, her face on that occasion displayed " a radiance such as I have seldom seen." A photographer captured the moment and the photograph went round the world. In vivid contrast, years later, was the deep grief which showed as she trudged through the stricken Welsh village of Aberfan.

In public, stirred by that same mystique of monarchy which stirs many of those who watch her, she is moved more easily to tears than laughter. There were tears in her eyes as she drove to her coronation. And there have been many occasions since when it has been a struggle to hold them back. Opening the Australian Parliament she was noticeably close to tears as Prime Minister John Menzies said, " You are in your own country. Among your own people. We are all yours—all parties, all creeds." In Canada, on another occasion, a crowd of small cheering children caused her noticeably to swallow as her eyes filmed over and her fingers twisted the strap of her handbag into emotional knots.

At times, the monarch in her can be impatient of attempts to treat her as a mere woman, as Harold Macmillan discovered when he tried to dissuade her from visiting Ghana. The place was in a state of unrest at the time. " Not suitable for a woman," Macmillan advised her (or words to that effect). The Queen's reply to that was that she was not going to Ghana as a woman, but as the monarch.

Yet in the privacy of her palace home she is woman enough to treat Philip always as head of the family. And the double life she leads, as monarch on the one hand, wife and mother on the other, is shot through with similar anomalies.

As a woman she is happiest in casual clothes, comfortable tweeds, " sensible " shoes, a time-tested raincoat if the weather is bad. As monarch she has had to become accustomed to what Prince Charles once referred to, rather irreverently, as " dressing up and queening it." The first time she saw her royal regalia laid out for her to wear she was almost horrified. She could not possibly wear all that, she said. She may not have said that it was too " showy "—though she has said more than once since that she does not want to look like a movie star—but she implied that it was.

" Oh, but you must, Your Majesty," her dresser informed her. " It is expected of you."

For her workaday life about the palace, the Queen compromises by wearing a comparatively simple, though not necessarily inexpensive, dress, perhaps silk or cotton in summer, wool in winter, with a few favourite pieces of jewellery, the pearls her grandparents gave her to mark their own Silver Jubilee, matching pearl ear-studs which were another gift from Queen Mary, a sapphire and diamond brooch handed down from Queen Victoria (who had it as a wedding gift from Prince Albert) and a gold and platinum wristwatch which was a gift from France.

The wristwatch, in fact, is the second of its kind. The first was lost at Sandringham in circumstances which must seem unusual to those who think of her only as monarch. It was surely the woman rather than a monarch who took her dogs out ratting one day, removed her gloves in order to handle them better and somehow lost her watch in the process. Days of searching by Boy Scouts, police, soldiers with mine detectors and members of the public failed to find it and it was left to the French, when they heard what had happened, to present her with an exact duplicate.

The Queen's day starts at eight o'clock in the morning. Weekdays or weekends, working days or holidays, she is always called at eight. The only exception is if she is on a royal tour and has a particular early engagement. Then she is called even earlier.

The day starts with breakfast, a read of the newspapers, a look through her personal correspondence. She is not the voluminous letter-writer Queen Victoria was. On the contrary, she has a habit of letting her personal mail accumulate and then clearing as much as possible in a hurried spate of letter-writing with a gold-topped pen.

She works in what used to be her mother's sitting-room. It is now a multi-purpose room—study, sitting-room, family room. Philip has the King's old room, though it is no longer the high-ceilinged, old-fashioned sanctum it was once. With a false ceiling to give it a more streamlined appearance, curtains that open or close at the press of a button, with its remote-controlled tape recorder and television set, it has long since been converted into the efficient working headquarters of a professional prince who, these days, is frequently busier than his wife.

To the casual eye, the desk at which the Queen works might seem cluttered. Prominent among the mass of articles which crowd it are those things which dominate the Queen's life, a rotary calendar and a brass carriage clock, a framed list of the day's appointments and a loose-leaf book listing future engagements. There are two telephones, one for conversations which are secret or confidential enough to require scrambling. There is a silver inkstand and a leather-bound rack holding scarlet-crested notepaper. A leather-bound blotter which matches the rack is flanked by a notebook and a tray containing pencils. Another tray holds paper clips, pins and rubber bands. There is a glass bowl containing a moist sponge (for sticking down envelopes), a pot of paste and a stick of wax in case any document requires the royal seal. Overlooking all this is an adjustable desk lamp and ranged along the back of the desk is a batch of framed photographs, including the first photo of himself Philip ever gave the Queen, another of the two of them on their honeymoon, one of Charles as a baby and others of the Queen Mother and the late Queen Mary.

At the side of the desk, within easy reach, is a small side-table. On it stands the first of the day's dispatch boxes. These are the famous boxes which pursue the Queen wherever she goes as they have pursued all British monarchs of recent generations. They follow her to Balmoral in summer, to Windsor at Christmas, to Sandringham over New Year. The contents, though not the actual boxes, are flown out to her if she is away on an overseas tour.

The Queen unlocks the box and goes through the contents. These may include Cabinet papers, Foreign Office telegrams, communications from countries of the Commonwealth. Some are for information only; others require her approval, signature and royal seal. " Drudgery," the late Duke of Windsor called this side of royal work when he was Edward VIII. There is no way of knowing how the Queen looks at it. But she tackles it dutifully and conscientiously.

She rings for her Private Secretary to advise on and assist with the contents of the box. The Private Secretary brings with him other documents with which she must also deal, perhaps the draft of a speech the Queen will make later that week, perhaps the preliminaries of yet another royal tour, perhaps more correspondence. With the exception of those from obvious fruit-and-nut cases, like the woman who at one time wrote more or less regularly claiming to be England's true queen, the Queen sees all letters addressed to her. People with grievances sometimes write to her as a sort of Court of Last Resort. She may not, perhaps cannot, intervene directly, but she usually passes the letter on to the appropriate ministry with a request that the matter is looked into.

Such a request from the Queen is not far short of a royal

command, as Ken Dolan, a rifleman in the Light Infantry, was delighted to discover. Having already changed the date of his wedding once (in order to qualify for married quarters when he was posted to Hong Kong), soldier Dolan found himself faced with the necessity for altering it yet again because of an un-expected five-week spell of training in Canada. The bride-to-be's father appealed to the Queen. The family " could not afford to keep changing the day," he said in his letter. The Queen passed the letter on to the Defence Secretary, with the result that Dolan was permitted to remain behind and get married when his regiment flew out to Canada.

The Queen's Private Secretary is usually followed by either the Deputy P.S. or Assistant P.S., perhaps both, with more documents, more letters, to be studied, answered, approved. But the Queen, as her Private Secretary pointed out to the 1971 Select Committee, is a housewife as well as a monarch. So once a month at least she must go over the household accounts with the Keeper of the Privy Purse. Once a week, on average, she must see the Master of the Household who will perhaps bring with him the book in which is listed any valuables which have been broken, chipped or gone astray. Breakages are rare; missing items even rarer, though there was one occasion, following a state banquet, when a gold fork was missing. However, it had not been taken by some thoughtless guest as a souvenir of the occasion. It had been inadvertently scraped into one of the garbage bins and was later recovered.

One or more of the royal corgis is never far away while the Queen works. There are six of them at the time this book is being written. Correction. There are four thoroughbred corgis— Heather, Brush, Pickles and Tinker. The other two royal pets, Shadow and Smoky, are the offspring of a liaison between one of the Queen's corgis and a dachshund belonging to Princess Margaret.

The morning's paperwork completed, it is time to move on. But first the Queen, because she is also a woman, opens her hand-bag, brings out the combined lipstick-powder compact which her inventive husband designed for her and freshens her make-up.

The tail-end of the morning sometimes finds her presiding over a meeting of the Privy Council. There are about twenty such meetings in the course of the average year. Usually they are held at Buckingham Palace, though they have also been held at Windsor, at Balmoral and Sandringham when the Queen has been on holiday there, aboard the royal yacht and even at Goodwood when the Queen was staying there for the races.

The complete list of the Privy Council totals over three hundred names. It includes Prince Philip, who was appointed by the Queen's father in 1951, all members of the Cabinet, representatives of the Commonwealth, the Archbishop of Canterbury and senior members of the Royal Household. But only three of the three hundred are required for a quorum and only those concerned with the immediate business in hand are usually summoned. It is one of the quaint traditions of British life that the business of the Privy Council is always transacted standing.

More frequently the tail-end of the morning will find the Queen in the first-floor Audience Room, just round the corner from her private apartment. Over the next sixty to ninety minutes she will receive in Audience perhaps eight or nine different people, allocating each of them about ten minutes of her time. New ambassadors and ministers taking up their posts at the sixty-odd embassies and legations in London present their credentials to her. Britain's own ambassadors report back briefly on their return from foreign parts. The waiting list on a particular morning may include an archbishop or bishop, governor or governor-general, a new or retiring judge, a field marshal or an air marshal, the president of a charitable organization or one of the top brass of the civil service. The spectrum is wide and varied.

The Queen stands to greet each visitor in turn before motioning him or her to one of the two armchairs in the room. She herself usually sits on the sofa. With many of her visitors, thanks to a preliminary briefing from her aides, she will talk knowledgeably enough, if briefly. She is less good when it comes to casual chit-chat and conversation on such occasions can become a little strained, flea-hopping perhaps from corgis to cattle to the education of royal princes as she strives to find common ground with the visitor of the moment. " Fairly forced " is how one V.I.P. recalls one such conversation. But should the visitor share her own enthusiasm for racehorses, then there is nothing forced about the resulting conversation. Indeed, time flies by unheeded as the Queen talks vivaciously and at length.

Sometimes a particularly important visitor—like Canada's

Pierre Trudeau—will be invited to stay on for lunch. Sometimes a whole batch of guests will have been invited along to what is known in royal circles as an " informal " luncheon party, though it is hardly as informal as all that.

Such luncheon parties are one of the very few innovations of the Queen's reign; there was nothing like them in her father's day. In a sense, they are " business " lunches, laid on to enable the Queen to meet and talk with a cross-section of national interests. Over the years since their inauguration, the guest list has perhaps tended to be dominated by politicians, trade unionists, civil servants and ecclesiastics, but there has also been a fair sprinkling of others, a surgeon and a fire chief, a hospital matron and the headmistress of a girls' school, a lawyer and a TV commentator, a painter or two, the odd author, actor and film star, even a pop star.

The guest list for one such luncheon, at Windsor Castle in April 1975, was fairly typical. Among those who sat down with the Queen and Prince Philip in their private dining-room were Beryl Grey of the Festival Ballet, playwright Alan Ayckbourn, cricketer Mike Denness, actor Arthur Lowe of *Dad's Army* fame, former pentathlon champion Jeremy Fox, Lord Catto, Sir Alexander Ross (chairman of the British Commonwealth Games Federation) and David Sanders (president of the Ship and Boat Builders Federation).

Guests usually number less than a dozen. More than that and conversation would become difficult. At Buckingham Palace they assemble in the Bow Room, where sherry and martinis are handed round. A scamper of corgis into the room heralds the arrival of the Queen, usually accompanied by Philip, the Prince of Wales or some other member of the family. The Queen Mother, for instance, joined that 1975 luncheon at Windsor. Philip will join the guests in a pre-lunch drink. The Queen may have a sherry, but more often settles for orange squash.

After half an hour of ice-breaking conversation, the Palace Steward announces that luncheon is served and the Queen leads the way into the adjoining 1844 Room. The luncheon table is oval. The Queen sits not at one end but midway along with Philip facing her. In this way, they can more easily encourage conversation with guests on either side. The corgis make themselves comfortable under the table. The meal usually runs to four courses, starting with melon or prawn cocktail and ending with cheese and fresh fruit. Afterwards comes coffee and a choice of brandy or liqueurs. Cigars and cigarettes are handed round, though neither the Queen nor Prince Philip smoke. Lunch over, everyone moves back into the Bow Room where conversation continues a while longer until the Queen goes round shaking hands as a sign that the get-together is over.

But such luncheon parties—perhaps four to eight of them in an average year—are the exception rather than the rule. Frequently the Queen lunches alone. Philip, with his own busy round of public engagements, is often not in for lunch.

Over the years, the pattern of the Queen's personal life has changed perhaps more than that of her public life, as is the way of things in most families. Anne has married and has a home of her own. Charles too has virtually left home though he has a bachelor pad at the palace for use when on leave from the Navy or when royal engagements require his presence in London. Andrew and Edward are away at boarding school for much of the year.

So busy is Philip these days that he is sometimes not home even for dinner at night; indeed, he is sometimes away, flipping about the world, for days on end. The Queen does not mind. She is a woman who, away from the public limelight, can be quite content with her own company. Of an evening, in any event, there is usually some additional work to fill part of the time, letters, gift photographs or Christmas cards (several hundred each year) to be signed. That done, there are the evening papers to leaf through, crossword puzzles to be tackled assiduously, television to be watched.

The Queen is a selective viewer; not an addict. She enjoys programmes of any sort involving horses—racing, show jumping, even *Black Beauty*—and wildlife programmes like *Survival*. Major sporting events like the Olympic Games and World Cup football appeal to her if Britain is taking part. Historical or biographical programmes about her ancestors or relatives naturally have a special appeal. She altered the time of the evening meal to free herself to watch *The Life and Times of Earl Mountbatten* and was disappointed when one of her Windsor Castle dinner parties during Royal Ascot caused her to miss that week's instalment of *Edward VII*. However, we understand that the episode was video-taped and she caught up with it later. She likes both a good laugh and a play with a real plot. But she does not care much for those abstruse plays-with-a-message which the high-brows of television push at viewers so frequently.

" Oh, it's one of those," she will say if she happens to switch on by mistake, and off goes the royal television set.

Monday afternoons, following the Queen's return from her weekend at Windsor or Sandringham, are kept free for her hair-dresser. Ahead of a royal tour, other afternoons are often taken up with dress fittings. Yet more afternoons are given over to public engagements in or near London.

The Queen's engagement diary for a recent twelve-month period gives some idea of what she does apart from paperwork.* In the course of what was more or less an average year the Queen held four luncheon parties, four garden parties at Buckingham Palace and another at Holyroodhouse in Edinburgh, seven investitures (a single investiture can involve shaking hands with perhaps 150-200 people) and presided over some twenty meetings of the Privy Council. She gave nearly three hundred Audiences, twenty of them to the prime minister. She held receptions for members of the Diplomatic Corps, delegates to the North Atlantic Assembly, Commonwealth officials meeting in London and holders of the Victoria and George Crosses.

She visited Renfrewshire, Newcastle, Bradford, Halifax, Maidenhead and Windsor (the town, not the castle). She visited the Royal Air Force at Finningley, the Grenadier Guards at Windsor, the South of England Agricultural Show, the Churchill centenary exhibition, Wellington College in Berkshire, Queen Elizabeth's College at Greenwich, the submarine base at Faslane, the Commonwealth Institute, the Royal College of Defence Studies, the I.B.M. plant at Havant, a steel works at Scunthorpe, Edinburgh Academy and Register House, Edinburgh. She also visited the Game Fair at Stratfield Saye, home of the Duke of Wellington, with an escort of some three hundred reporters and photographers who hoped the visit might foreshadow further developments in the rumoured romance between the Prince of Wales and the Duke's daughter, Lady Jane Wellesley.

She saw the oil rig *Ocean Kokuei* and inspected oil installations

* Appendix I.

at Nigg Bay. She inspected the newly electrified rail system
between Preston and Glasgow, travelling part of the way in the
driver's cab. She took the salute at a parade of Queen's Scouts
and presented new colours to both the Parachute Regiment and
the Royal Military Academy. She inspected the Yeomen of the
Guard and the new décor of the Albert Hall. She opened a new
fire service college at Moreton in the Marsh, new police headquarters in Edinburgh, a new medical school in Southampton
and the new home of the Royal Academy of Dancing. She dined
with the Lord Mayor of London and attended a garden party
given by the Irish Guards. She went to receptions given by the
Royal Society of Arts, the Imperial Society of Knights Bachelor,
the King George Jubilee Trust and the Royal Auxiliary Air
Force.

She attended special services in St Paul's Cathedral, St Giles'
Cathedral, Edinburgh, Hexham Abbey and the Royal Garrison
Church of All Saints at Aldershot. She went to two film premières
and saw the Scottish Opera Company perform *The Merry
Widow*. She went to the Derby, the Chelsea Flower Show, the
Royal Tournament and the International Horse Show. She
opened Parliament, took the salute at the Trooping the Colour,
distributed the Royal Maundy (the service was held that year in
Salisbury Cathedral), attended both the British Legion Festival
of Remembrance and the Remembrance Day service at the
Cenotaph.

It was also a year in which she again visited Australia and
New Zealand as Queen of those countries. She had been back
from Canberra only twelve days when she was taking off again,
this time on a state visit to Indonesia. At the same time she also
visited Bali, the Cook Islands, the Solomon Islands, Norfolk
Island, the New Hebrides and New Guinea, each place with its
own separate schedule of public engagements. She played hostess
to the Queen of Denmark and the elected King of Malaysia on
their state visits to Britain.

It was a year in which, as with every other year since 1952,
she had to be all things to all people; regal without being imperious, glamorous without being sexy, dutiful but not dull,
religious but not priggish, modest but not prudish, reserved without betraying her inherent shyness. It is a difficult, perhaps impossible, task. In an age when ancient loyalties are more divided

The Princess, aged ten,
with her family at the
Welsh House, Royal Lodge,
Windsor

Before going for a ride at
Windsor on her thirteenth
birthday

Learning to tie a knot as a Girl Guide

The Princess changes a wheel during training at an A.T.S. centre in 1945

than they once were, it is also a tightrope the Queen continues to walk with considerable skill.

She is perhaps not helped by some of the things written about her and some of the often strange things done in her name. A spot of spring-cleaning when the Queen is expected is as understandable as a spot of tidying-up at home before guests arrive. But Government departments, local councils and nationalized industries often seem to suffer a distinct rush of royal blood to the head.

In Manchester on one occasion, for instance, they not only repaired the broken window of a slum cottage with hardboard but painted artificial curtains on the hardboard. And the Queen was not even visiting the cottage; simply driving past.

Elsewhere in Lancashire, a horde of workmen descended on a small railway station near Wigan, giving it its first paint job in twenty years, repairing roofs, replacing flagstones and erecting a new fence . . . all because the royal train was scheduled to make a two-minute stop.

At Stirling the two " Gentlemen " signs on the platform were removed ahead of the Queen's visit in case they offended royal eyes. In Essex, when the Queen was expected, a hot-dog stand was ordered to close for the day and cover up its " Juicy Hot Dogs " slogan. Perhaps they thought the Queen might have the royal corgis with her! In London's East End a mechanical sweeper and a convoy of trucks were called in to clear a local rubbish tip when it was learned that the Queen was visiting a nearby toy factory.

Nor is this sort of blood-to-the-head business by any means confined to Britain. In Stuttgart, ahead of the Queen's visit, they rushed around spraying the local grass with green fluid to conceal any bare patches.

Deification also embraces others of the Royal Family. One local council, expecting the Queen Mother, had a false wall installed to conceal the fact that their guildhall possessed such a thing as a loo. At Exeter, to enable Philip to get a good night's rest aboard the royal train, a branch line was closed down and five trains cancelled. To get local commuters to work, British Rail, despite its other loss-making activities, laid on a fleet of buses and taxis.

Neither the Queen nor Philip are necessarily deceived by such

C

antics. The Queen's eyes were first opened to what goes on in the name of royalty when she did a brief wartime stint in the A.T.S. and her unit was inspected by her aunt, the Princess Royal.

"What a business it has been," she grumbled to Princess Margaret afterwards. "Spit and polish all day long. Now I know what goes on when Mummy and Papa go anywhere."

Today, she usually sees the funny side of such antics. Philip is more likely to see the dangers. "Creating traffic jams to give royal cars a clear passage is the quickest way of turning loyalists into republicans," he commented once.

Philip is right, of course. Those who deify the Royals to such a ridiculous extent do the monarchy more harm than people like Willie Hamilton, who has said that he would lose no sleep if the monarchy ended tomorrow. His argument, if we understand it correctly, is that tradition could still be maintained without the Queen.

But could it?

Would the Maundy money be the same if it was dished out by some archbishop? Would the Trooping the Colour be the same with some field marshal taking the salute? Would Ascot be the same with President Brand X driving down the course instead of the Queen?

The prime minister, of course, could just as easily read the Speech from the Throne at the annual opening of Parliament. It is, after all, his speech, setting out the Government programme. The Queen merely reads it.

Theoretically, the Queen may be head of everything—the State, the Church; the fountain of both justice and honour. The government of the day is always Her Majesty's Government, Cabinet ministers are her ministers, state departments her agents and civil servants her servants. Every Act of Parliament is theoretically enacted in her name and becomes law only when she has given her royal assent. The armed forces serve her—theoretically—and not the state which pays them. The practice is very different. The Queen cannot refuse to assent to anything which Parliament has determined. In constitutional matters she can act only on the advice of the government. In short, she reigns but she does not rule.

Yet she is much more than a civil servant with a crown on her head, as she was slightingly referred to during the course of one

House of Commons debate. How much more was seen in Mexico only a day before that tag was applied to her in the Commons. In Mexico City more than a million people packed the streets, bringing her car to a halt and bombarding her with so many flowers that she was knee-deep in them by the time she reached her hotel. No president gets that sort of welcome.

What, then, does the Queen's work add up to? Is she no more than a royal rubber stamp, approving only what others have decided, or a royal soporific, serving the same purpose in Britain as religion serves in some Latin American countries?

She is surely more than that.

There are no available statistics to show what she and Philip, between them, may have accomplished over the years of monarchy in cementing good relations, smoothing out differences, bolstering Britain's dwindling prestige. Such things are not capable of being computerized. But was it merely coincidence that Anglo-American relations, severely strained by the Suez crisis, took a fresh upward turn after a royal visit to the United States? Was it coincidence that Britain's exports to the United States, France, the Netherlands, increased after visits to those countries by Prince Philip?

The Queen and her husband would be the last to claim any credit. They can only " create an atmosphere," as Philip has said. The rest is done by politicians and businessmen.

But in matters of international relations and trade, " atmosphere " is the all-important first ingredient. And history, looking back and seeing things in proper perspective, may decide that the Queen, through her world travels or in the privacy of the blue-and-white Audience Room at Buckingham Palace, accomplished more than anyone understood or appreciated at the time.

2

Childhood

The baby destined to become Queen Elizabeth II was born on
21st April 1926 in one of those elegant Georgian mansions which,
like the barrel organs, open-topped buses and horse-drawn drays
of the period, gave London a lingering atmosphere of old-world
charm.

Looking back, it must sometimes seem to the Queen that she
was born into an entirely different world, so great has been the
change over the last fifty years. In those days of the 1920s the
motor-car was still a luxury and no one dreamed that it would
one day become a menace. Television was still in the future and
radio in its infancy. Films were silent, awaiting the arrival of Al
Jolson in *The Jazz Singer* the following year. In London audiences were flocking to see the latest film of a great little actor on
whom the newborn princess was to bestow a knighthood nearly
half a century later for his services to art. The film was *The Gold
Rush* and the star was Charlie Chaplin.

But in one respect things were much the same then as now.
Britain was going through a period of economic and social stress.
It was the year of the General Strike.

It was also the year in which Rudolph Valentino died. Ten
cigarettes cost the equivalent of two pence in today's decimalized
and devalued coinage. Whisky was sixty pence a bottle. A small
turkey cost less than a bottle of whisky, though there were many
who could afford neither. Rabbit was to be the main dish in many
working-class homes the following Christmas.

It was an era when girls had cupid-bow lips that looked as
though they were smeared with raspberry jam, wore their hair
cropped or in a fringe, decked themselves out in fancy garters,
imitation slave bangles and monkey-fur coats. " Ripping " and

" topping " were favourite expressions among the bright young things and the Charleston was all the rage.

The British Empire was at the peak of its greatness and the bearded father-figure of King George V looked down benevolently from the throne.

The baby born in Bruton Street was the King's first granddaughter and her birth was saluted by the thunder of twenty-one guns in Hyde Park. The baby's father, Albert, Duke of York, was a slim, pleasantly nervous young man of thirty with a slight speech impediment.

" You'll be lucky if she'll have you," his father had warned him gruffly when he declared his intention of proposing to Elizabeth Bowes-Lyon, popular daughter of the fourteenth Earl of Strathmore and Kinghorne. To the surprise of both—and her own, as she confessed later—she accepted him.

They had been married for three years and were certainly not to be classed among the bright young things of the period. They much preferred to stay home at nights even though they did not yet have a settled home of their own. As a result, the house in which the future Queen was born was the London home of her maternal grandfather. The baby's mother was twenty-five at the time and, in accordance with tradition, the Home Secretary held a watching brief in an adjoining room to ensure that no changeling was introduced into the royal line.

As the King's grand-daughter, the baby was christened in the private chapel at Buckingham Palace, swaddled in a christening robe of Honiton lace which her father, grandfather and great-grandfather (Edward VII) had all worn before her. She was given the names Elizabeth Alexandra Mary. Elizabeth was her mother's name; Mary came from her grandmother, Queen Mary; Alexandra was the name of her grandfather's Danish-born mother, Queen Alexandra, widow of Edward VII, who had died only five months before at the age of eighty-one.

It was a birth which materially affected the order of succession to the throne. Until then, the King's sons—the Prince of Wales, the Dukes of York, Gloucester and Kent—had been the first four in the line of succession. With the exception of the baby's father, all were still unmarried. But now Gloucester and Kent found themselves pushed a step further down the ladder of succession, with the baby known as Lilibet in the family circle (after her early attempts to pronounce her own name) third in line after her uncle, the universally popular Prince of Wales, and her own father. At the time, the change seemed relatively unimportant. Few thought that the natural order of things would ever permit her to actually succeed to the throne.

Her Uncle David, the Prince of Wales and next in line, was young, healthy and good-looking. At thirty-one, there was still plenty of time for him to marry and have children of his own. Even if he did not, her own parents could well have other children, and boys, if they came along, would take precedence over her, a mere girl, as Andrew and Edward take precedence over Princess Anne today.*

Yet there was perhaps one person who did visualize circumstances in which Elizabeth Alexandra Mary might one day succeed to the throne—her grandmother, Queen Mary.

Queen Mary knew from sad and bitter experience that death as well as birth can sometimes deal a hand in the game of royal succession. More than half a century before, as Princess May of Teck, a girl in her twenties, she had been betrothed to the prince who, had he lived, would have succeeded to the throne as Albert I, Albert Victor or Edward VIII, according to whichever name he decided to take. A matter of weeks before the date set for their marriage, he was taken ill at Sandringham. Within five days he was dead. Eighteen months later she married his brother. Now the brother was King and she was Queen.†

Of course, she can hardly have visualized the Abdication. Such a thing, at the time, was completely foreign to her own strict rules of royal conduct. But she visualized . . . something. If not then, certainly four years later when, with the Prince of Wales still unmarried, the Yorks had not a son but another daughter. With Margaret's birth, the old Queen—she was sixty-three at the time—decided that the time had come when it might be wise to start training the elder of her two small grand-daughters along the path of possible monarchy.

It was Queen Mary who gave the girl who is now the Queen her first lesson in acknowledging the cheers of the crowd. She was five at the time and the occasion was her grandfather's Birth-

---

* Appendix II.
† The full story is told in our book *Bertie and Alix*.

day Parade. It was Queen Mary too, when Elizabeth first started lessons, who helped governess Marion Crawford to draw up what was regarded as a suitable curriculum. Not too much arithmetic; the child was hardly likely to need that. Plenty of history though, so that she should know all about her heritage. And poetry—so good for training the memory.

Grandmother, in fact, took over part of the curriculum, one afternoon a week being set aside for what was noted down as " Educational visit with Queen Mary." Obediently and happily Elizabeth trotted alongside as her stiff-backed imperious grandmother whisked her round museums, art galleries and like places of historic interest.

There is a story that one of these visits was to the Royal Tournament. As the crowds surged round, the small Princess exclaimed excitedly, " Have they all come to see me?" So unregal a remark so shocked her grandmother that Queen Mary promptly bustled her off home again.

While we cannot vouch for the story, you can be sure that Queen Mary lost no opportunity of instilling in her granddaughter her own rigid ideas of royal behaviour, royal destiny and, above all, royal duty. Queen Mary may not have believed in the Divine Right of Kings (and Queens), but she assuredly believed that kings, queens and even small princesses should put royal duty before everything else.

That the future Queen, from quite an early age, was not entirely unaware of what might lie ahead of her is revealed in a childish remark made one day while watching riders in Rotten Row.

" If ever I am Queen," she piped up, " I shall make a law that there is no riding on Sundays. Horses need a rest too."

She was about six at the time, with the abdication which was to make her heiress presumptive still some years in the future. Where, then, did she get the idea that she might one day be Queen? It can only have been from her grandmother.

Certainly it was not from her parents. They had no thought in those days that they might one day be King and Queen and would have been horrified if anyone had suggested it.

The Yorks, parents and children, constituted a warm and loving family. The childhood years of the future Queen Elizabeth II were happy and secure ones which the Queen, looking back, recalls as " a time when the sun always seemed to be shining."

From morning till night, the tall narrow house at 145 Piccadilly, into which the Yorks moved soon after Elizabeth's birth, echoed with laughter and squeals of childish delight. The day started with Elizabeth and Margaret scuttling into their parents' bedroom for an early-morning romp; ended with splashing in the bathroom and pillow fights at bedtime. In between came walks in Hyde Park or Kensington Gardens with governess Marion Crawford or nurserymaid Margaret Macdonald, the beloved " Bobo " who later became the Queen's Dresser. There were outings in an open carriage which Grandpapa sent round from Buckingham Palace and games of hopscotch and hide-and-seek in Hamilton Gardens in which the girls' father sometimes joined. Their mother, prior to the arrival of Miss Crawford, taught Lilibet to read, as she was later to teach her own children in turn. Of an evening, in those pre-television days, parents and children would play card games like snap and happy families.

Uncle David, a frequent caller at the York house, would sometimes join in, finding it easy to relax in the informal atmosphere of his brother's home. Sometimes the Allendale children would come in from next door or there would be a visit from Lilibet's cousins, Gerald and George Lascelles. There were carefree weekends at Royal Lodge, the country house at Windsor which George V had given his son and daughter-in-law; holidays at Birkhall, a shooting lodge on the Balmoral estate, or at Glamis, the Bowes-Lyon ancestral home where there were marvellous " dressing up " chests crammed with the fashions of a previous generation. These chests became a memory of childhood which were to remain with Elizabeth down the years and when, years later, she became a mother herself, she saw to it that her children had a similar " dressing up " chest in the nursery at Buckingham Palace.

While most small girls adore dolls, Elizabeth doted on horses. At one time there were as many as thirty toy horses " stabled " on the landing outside her top-floor nursery. With Margaret's help, she would unsaddle them at night, groom them and pretend to feed them. A toy farm was another childhood enthusiasm to be added to over the years. Additional lead animals were usually bought at Woolworths because that was where her pocket money went furthest and even today, as Queen, she still has a strong economic streak built in her during those shilling-a-week days of childhood. Today, clothes made for overseas tours must be worn up at less important functions back home and a lost dog lead must be assiduously hunted for until found again. " Dog leads cost money," she told Charles once when he lost one.

In the York household, in the days of the Queen's childhood, money was certainly not thrown about. Clothes (cotton dresses and tweed coats) were plain and serviceable; shoes sensible and hard-wearing. Her only item of jewellery until she was ten was a broken pearl and coral necklace belonging to her mother. She disliked milk puddings, but was made to eat them because they were " good " for her. Pocket money seldom stretched to sweets. Instead, there were handfuls of coffee crystals which she sorted carefully into piles, according to size, while Margaret was busy stuffing hers straight in her mouth.

Margaret was the impatient, impulsive one. Lilibet was serious and methodical (but also the one with the temper). Ribbons from chocolate boxes were as carefully folded and hoarded as foreign stamps are peeled from incoming mail and kept today. Gifts received for Christmas or birthdays must be listed and then ticked off as thank-you letters were written.

A small room off the main drawing-room at 145 Piccadilly served as schoolroom. Here, from half-past nine to eleven each morning, and at Royal Lodge on Saturday mornings, she tackled English literature, grammar, writing and composition, history (which she liked) and geography (which she did not), arithmetic, poetry and Bible study. French was added later. Lessons were followed by games in Hamilton Gardens or a short walk.

She was seven when she was first accompanied on her morning walk by a small, foxy-looking dog. " What on earth is that?" people asked each other. It was, of course, the first of the royal corgis, nicknamed Dookie.

After her morning walk she had to rest and read until lunch-time. *Black Beauty* was a favourite book and the occasional ' comic ' afforded light relief. Aboard the royal train at Euston station one day, awaiting the arrival of her parents, she tapped on the window to attract the attention of a policeman, handed him her weekly shilling and asked him to buy her some ' comics ' from the station bookstall.

In the afternoons, except when she was off on an " educational visit with Queen Mary," there were music, singing, dancing and art lessons. There were attempts to teach her knitting and needle-work, but, to Queen Mary's disappointment, she was no good at either. Her hands were far better at handling a horse's reins and on Saturdays, at Windsor, came the weekly lesson to which she looked forward more than any other. This was a riding lesson on the Shetland pony which was a gift from grandfather George V.

But if the Queen's young life was warm, happy and secure, as it assuredly was, it was also cloistered and coddled, very different from the sort of upbringing which, years later, she was to accord her own children. For her, there were no years of boarding school to round off—or perhaps create—a few rough edges, no outside circle of friends and acquaintances, no childhood jaunts to Euro-pean countries; only lessons from her governess, friends from within the small tight royal circle, regular-as-clockwork visits to Glamis and Birkhall. There was, however, a once-in-a-lifetime stay at the seaside, at Eastbourne, where she built sandcastles, collected seashells and rode donkeys on the sands. She stayed with her parents at a house lent to them by the Duke of Devon-shire. Arriving, they found on the hall table a large, half-com-pleted jigsaw left out so that anyone with a few minutes to spare could add a few more pieces. It was another memory to be stored away and brought out again in the future, as Mark Phillips found out when he went to Sandringham for the first time and found himself whiling away the odd minutes with a similar jigsaw.

While she herself may not have realized it, her childhood outings, to such things as the Horse Show and the Royal Tourna-ment, were extremely circumscribed. A ride on top of a double decker bus was a never-to-be-repeated treat. There was a similar once-only trip on the London Underground.

She was a bridesmaid at the wedding of her uncle, the Duke of Kent (who married Princess Marina) and, a year later, at that of another uncle, the Duke of Gloucester (who married Alice Montagu-Douglas-Scott, daughter of the Duke of Buccleuch). Because both uncles were junior to her father, any children they might have would not displace her in the order of succession.

At nine there was a carriage drive to St Paul's to celebrate her grandfather's Silver Jubilee. The pearl necklace the Queen wears so frequently today is the one he gave her to commemorate the occasion. But within a year Grandpapa was dead and Uncle David was King Edward VIII, still unmarried and without children. She was now second in the line of succession and events were in train, even if she was too young to realize and understand, which were to bring her a further step closer to the throne.

Among members of the Royal Family, though not to the children of course, it was no longer a secret that the new King was emotionally involved with an attractive American divorcee. He brought her to have tea one afternoon with the Yorks.

" Who is she?" Elizabeth wanted to know.

"A friend of Uncle David's," she was doubtless told, as children are usually fobbed off in such awkward circumstances.

How much she understood of the constitutional and emotional crisis which followed it is impossible to know. Probably very little. She was only ten and young for her years, as most girls of her generation were.

To her, 10th December 1936, for the most part, was a day much like any other. Lessons in the morning; piano practice in the afternoon. The only difference was that her mother was ill in bed with a heavy cold.

As she tinkered away at her scales, the young Elizabeth may not have known that at Windsor Uncle David had signed the Instrument of Abdication, that her father was now King George VI and that she was the next Monarch. The faint possibility which her grandmother, Queen Mary, had visualized all those years before had finally come to pass.

3

Royal Apprenticeship

Among the callers at 145 Piccadilly that December day in 1936, when Edward VIII became Duke of Windsor and his brother succeeded him as King, was Queen Mary. As regally dutiful as ever, she came to make obeisance to her sick daughter-in-law who was now Queen, just as, years later, she was among the first to curtsy to her grand-daughter when she became Queen Elizabeth II.

It was perhaps from her grandmother, perhaps from her governess, that the young Elizabeth first learned of the big change in her own life. By that evening she already knew and understood sufficient to remark " That's Mummy now, isn't it?" when she spotted a letter addressed to " Her Majesty the Queen " lying on a side table in the hall.

It was certainly Queen Mary who took the girl who was now Heiress Presumptive to witness the colourful ceremony at which her father was proclaimed King. (' Presumptive ' instead of ' Apparent ' because it was not beyond the bounds of possibility that her mother, still capable of child-bearing at thirty-six, might yet have a son to supplant her in the line of succession.)

Until a few weeks before neither of the girls' parents had visualized that they would one day be King and Queen. Neither of them really wanted it. Never very robust, completely untrained in monarchy, her father in particular felt himself unfitted for the task. Until now he had never even glimpsed the contents of the sacred dispatch boxes which were to pursue him throughout his reign, just as they had plagued his father before him and have continued to bombard his daughter during her own twenty-five years of monarchy. There were a few in high places who mumbled their agreement as to his unsuitability and would have preferred his younger brother, the Duke of Kent, as King. But untrained and relatively frail though he was, he brought to the task which confronted him such strength of character, such sense of duty, that when he died fifteen years later his daughter could say with truth that " millions " mourned for him as for a true and trusted friend.

Unfitted though he felt himself to be at the outset, he was determined to do " my best to clear up the inevitable mess." It was to be no easy task. With national loyalties divided, there was, in those pre-war days, the possibility, again to quote George VI's own words, that the fabric of monarchy might " crumble under the strain and shock of it all." That it did not speaks volumes for the man who took up the reins his brother had laid down.

Two days after the Abdication came the ceremony of Accession. With his speech impediment, it was a considerable ordeal for the new King. If his small daughter sensed the strain her father underwent, she may also have sensed her mother's determination.

" We must take what is coming to us and make the best of it," her mother said. " There are going to be great changes."

One of the changes was the move from 145 Piccadilly to Buckingham Palace. While Elizabeth had been there often enough to visit her grandparents when they were King and Queen, the idea of living in that vast impersonal edifice filled her with something akin to dismay.

" You mean for ever?" she exclaimed when told that the palace was to be her new home.

There were other changes in her young life. Until now, there had been no real degree of continuity between successive British monarchs. Queen Victoria thoroughly disapproved of the son who succeeded her as Edward VII and neglected to train him at all. There was, in turn, a wide gulf of misunderstanding between Edward and the son who succeeded him as George V. And George V stands condemned out of his own mouth. " My father was frightened of his mother. I was frightened of my father. And I'm damned well going to see to it that my children are frightened of me." They were, and the fact that they were perhaps had something to do with George VI's speech impediment.

The Queen's father was cast in a very different mould. He wanted his daughters to love him, not to be frightened of him.

Untrained and unfitted as he felt himself to be, he was determined that his elder daughter should not find herself in the same predicament when her time came.

So her training began. As the day of his coronation drew near, the King devised a special picture book for his daughter to explain the significance of the ceremony. Not to be outdone, Queen Mary produced from her collection of historical bygones a Victorian peepshow depicting the coronation of George IV.

Elizabeth's lessons were broadened to teach her something about lineage, dynasty and monarchy. Her father took her with him to Greenwich to open the National Maritime Museum and had her stand beside him for a march-past of Boy Scouts at Windsor. She stood with her parents at the head of the Grand Staircase in Buckingham Palace to welcome official guests. She was taught a short speech in French with which to greet President Lebrun of France when he arrived for the coronation.

Busy as he was with the new duties of monarchy, her father had less time for games like happy families and hopscotch. Elizabeth was upset by that, for she was still a child as well as Heiress Presumptive. The things of childhood still had a place in her young life. The toy horses which had been stabled on the landing at Piccadilly were now lined up along the nursery corridor in the palace. In company with the chubby, impulsive Margaret, Elizabeth explored the palace gardens, larger and more exciting than Hamilton Gardens at the rear of 145 Piccadilly. As winter gave way to spring that year of 1937, the summer house in the gardens became an outdoor schoolroom. There was a lake too where wild duck nested and reared their young. Scrambling about in search of a nest, Elizabeth overbalanced and fell in. She was pulled out dripping with green slime . . . much as her son, Charles, was to be lugged out of a sheep dip at Windsor covered with pink dye years later.

For the coronation her father had a small lightweight coronet made for her. She wore it with a lace dress, an ermine-trimmed cloak, short socks and silver sandals. The dress had a small train. Margaret's dress had no train and she worked herself into a bit of a tantrum about it.

For her part, Elizabeth was worried that Margaret might disgrace the family by dozing off during the ceremony. " You're very young for a coronation," she told her sister. Far from dozing off, Margaret made rather too much noise when the time came.

" I had to nudge her," Elizabeth informed her parents when they were all home again.

Latin was added to her lessons. Her reading was broadened to include Muzzey's *History of the United States* and Foucin's *Géographie Historique* as well as Chaucer and Keats, Scott and Dickens. She was taught to swim, ride a bicycle and play tennis. At swimming she gained a certificate for life-saving. At tennis she was less adept. " It's no good waiting for the ball to come to you. You must run for it," her coach told her.

By stages her pocket money was increased to five shillings a week. She saved some of it and by 1939, when she was thirteen, had a nest-egg of £30 in the Post Office savings bank.

She cut the cake at a tea for disabled ex-servicemen, presented the rosettes at the National Pony Show and took the salute at a rehearsal for the Aldershot Tattoo. She was sometimes allowed to stay up late and watch the guests arrive for a palace banquet. Queen Mary did not approve any more than Queen Victoria had approved of the late hours her eldest son and daughter-in-law permitted their children to keep.

The grandmother continued to play an active part in the grand-daughter's training. Every Monday afternoon the two of them set out together on some fresh educational excursion, to Westminster Abbey and the Tower of London, Greenwich Palace and Hampton Court, the National Gallery and the Wallace Collection. They visited museums galore (the British, the Science and the Victoria and Albert) as well as the Bank of England, the postal sorting office at Mount Pleasant and the Royal Mint.

Elizabeth watched her father open Parliament and accompanied her parents on a royal visit to Scotland. But when President Roosevelt suggested that she and Margaret should join their parents on a visit to the United States, her father demurred. " They are much too young," he wrote back.

To give her some small degree of contact with other girls of her own age, a special company of Girl Guides was formed at the palace. It was guiding in its most genteel form and at the first meeting most of the other girls turned up in party dresses. Elizabeth was horrified. She liked roughing it—as Charles does today—and she was in her element at weekends when, wearing her oldest clothes, she could help her father tackle the neglected, overgrown garden at Royal Lodge.

It does not seem to have occurred to either of her parents that she might benefit from proper schooling. Had it done so, Queen Mary would doubtless have disapproved. However, at the age of twelve she did start travelling back and forth to Eton College for private lessons in constitutional history and such abstruse subjects as the law of land tenure from the vice provost, Henry Marten.

She was thirteen in the July of 1939 when her father took her, along with her mother and sister, to visit the Royal Naval College at Dartmouth where he had once been a cadet. The full story of her meeting that day with Philip is told in our earlier book, *The Crown And The Ring*, and we will not recount it again here. Sufficient to say that for the adolescent Elizabeth it was a case of love at first sight.

From Dartmouth the family went on for their customary summer vacation at Balmoral. But as events in Europe moved towards a climax, the King and Queen were forced to return to London, leaving the two girls at Birkhall.

With the outbreak of war, Elizabeth found herself handing round tea and cakes at a weekly session organized to make comforts for the troops. She even tried her hand at knitting a pair of rather shapeless socks for some poor soldier. She followed what was happening in Europe by listening to the radio, though the voice of the renegade Lord Haw-Haw sometimes infuriated her to the extent of hurling a cushion or book at the radio set. Her lessons continued much as usual though constitutional history had to be done by correspondence. Each evening there was a telephone call from her parents.

During the period of what was known as the 'phoney' war it was decided that it was safe for her to return south. But not to Buckingham Palace. Instead, she and Margaret went to live at Royal Lodge, Windsor, where they followed the progress of the war with the aid of a large map and a supply of paper flags. Then suddenly the 'phoney' war erupted into violent reality.

As events moved towards the Battle of Britain, Elizabeth and Margaret were hurriedly switched from Royal Lodge to Windsor Castle. They were guarded by a hand-picked company of

Her last days as Princess.
Nairobi 1952,

At work in Buckingham
Palace

The Royal wedding of 1947

Grenadiers and there were secret instructions as to what was to be done with the two princesses if the Germans landed in Britain. Some royal advisers would have preferred the girls to have been sent immediately to Canada, but their mother would not hear of it.

" They can't possibly go without me," she said. " I cannot go without the King. And the King will never go."

So Elizabeth remained at Windsor, helping to collect scrap metal to boost aircraft production, picking peas in the fields and damsons in the orchard. She donned a Mickey Mouse gas mask for a mock gas attack, wrote letters of good cheer to royal servants now in the forces and knitted more shapeless socks. Another company of Girl Guides was formed. This time its members were not girls hand-picked from selected families. Many of them were wartime evacuees, Cockney kids from London to whom she was not Your Royal Highness, but plain " Lilibet." Being called by her pet name made her feel accepted, just as Charles, years later, was to feel accepted when schoolmates in Australia called him " you Pommy bastard."

The sound of bombs crumping down on London, twenty-three miles away, was heard often and at night flashes of anti-aircraft fire were visible beyond the blacked-out windows. The odd enemy bomber was seen overhead and there was a bell to warn of impending air raids. When that sounded at night the two princesses were supposed to dash down to the castle dungeons, pausing only to slip coats over their nightdresses. But the modest, fastidious Elizabeth insisted on " dressing properly." The length of time she took so worried those who had charge of her that finally they had " siren suits " made which she and Margaret could pop quickly over their nightwear.

Her birthplace in Bruton Street and her old home in Piccadilly were both destroyed by bombs. At their palace home her parents had a narrow escape. They were in their sitting-room overlooking the inner quadrangle when a German raider scored a direct hit on the palace with the King hustling the Queen to safety under the table only seconds before bombs blasted the quadrangle and the private chapel.

Despite the danger, Elizabeth's father insisted on remaining in London and throughout the war he and his wife continued to carry out public engagements at the staggering rate of some eight

D

hundred a year. It can hardly be wondered at that Elizabeth thought her mother looked " strained " and her father " grim " when they visited her at Windsor at weekends.

Conscious of the risk he was running by remaining in London, the King increased the momentum of his daughter's training. She was only fourteen when he first showed and explained to her the contents of the famous boxes.

Between father and daughter there existed not only the strongest possible bond of love and affection, but something else. A man who worked for the late King when the present Queen was still a girl told us once : " You could see it in their eyes whenever they looked at each other. I can't explain it, but it was there all right—a sort of special understanding."

There was one year when Marion Crawford, to ease the boredom and monotony of wartime life at Windsor, arranged for the princesses to take part in a nativity play called *The Christmas Child*. Margaret was the Child and Elizabeth one of the Three Kings. The sight of her in her make-believe crown touched some chord in her father so deeply that he cried as he watched.

For her part, she was never happier than when sitting with him, listening carefully as he explained some point of monarchy to her. There were other lessons which had nothing to do with monarchy, as the Queen revealed in Canada a few years back. There, to everyone's surprise, she joined enthusiastically in the tongue-twisting lyrics of *Susannah's A Funniful Man*.

" I learned it from my father," she explained afterwards. " He loved funny songs like that."

She made her first broadcast in a Children's Hour programme beamed also to the United States and Canada. She helped to draft the script and the last few words of the actual broadcast were her own spur-of-the-moment improvisation.

" My sister is at my side and we are both going to say good night to you," she said. Then, turning to Margaret, " Come on, Margaret."

" Good night," piped Margaret in a childish treble.

" Good night," echoed Elizabeth, " and good luck to you all."

At Badminton, where she was staying with the Duke and Duchess of Beaufort, Queen Mary listened to her grand-daughter with tears in her eyes.

Queen Mary travelled from Badminton to Windsor to be present when her grand-daughter was confirmed. On her sixteenth birthday, soon after, the Princess was made honorary colonel of the Grenadier Guards and took the salute at a birthday march-past. Wearing Girl Guide uniform, she also visited the local employment exchange at Windsor to register for war work. The event was well publicized, but no actual war work came her way. Her father felt that training for monarchy should come first.

At seventeen her father considered her sufficiently tutored to deputize for him when he was visiting British troops overseas. In consequence, he asked Parliament to amend the Regency Act under which Counsellors of State are appointed. He wanted his daughter, he said, to have " every opportunity of gaining experience in the duties which would fall upon her in the event of her acceding to the throne." Parliament agreed and amended the Act so that the Princess, instead of waiting until she was twenty-one, could deputize for her father from her eighteenth birthday. Soon after, when he set off to visit troops in Italy, she had her first experience of doing so.

In those less nationalistic days there were some who wanted her made Princess of Wales in celebration of her eighteenth birthday. Her father refused. In his view, that title was reserved for the wife of the Prince of Wales, even if at that time there was no Prince of Wales. Well, if she could not be Princess of Wales, suggested Edinburgh, why not Princess of Scotland? But the King would not have that either.

However, he took her with him to Wales to visit a tin-plate works at Newport, the docks at Swansea, the mining valleys and factories in South Wales. Later came a visit to Edinburgh where she accepted purses on behalf of the Scottish Y.W.C.A. She made her first public speech—to the governors of a children's hospital in Hackney—and it was perhaps a foretaste of things to come that she referred to her parents not as the King and Queen, but simply as " my father and mother."

She dined with Commonwealth prime ministers when they gathered in London, visited British, Canadian and U.S. air bases, launched the battleship *Vanguard* and, prior to D-Day, made a top-secret trip to watch a rehearsal of the parachute drops and glider landings which would spearhead the assault on Europe.

She pestered her father to allow her to do something which she could regard as " real war work."

" Look at what Mary's doing," she said to him on one occasion. Mary was Lady Mary Cambridge, a friend since nursery days, who was working as a nurse in the East End of London. " And I'm stuck here doing nothing."

Reluctantly her father gave way and she enrolled in the Auxiliary Territorial Service. It did not work out as perhaps she may have expected or wished. Her son, Prince Charles, during his spell in the navy, may consistently have undertaken the same duties and risks as any other young naval officer. It can hardly be said that the Queen, as Second Subaltern H.R.H. The Princess Elizabeth, did the same. The day she joined her Commanding Officer actually drove to Windsor to collect her. And each night, duty done, she returned to Windsor for dinner, bed and breakfast.

But if there were few hardships and no risks, she did at least learn to drive all types of vehicles, from staff cars to ambulances, and managed to get herself well smeared with grease while changing wheels and tinkering with engines. Back at Windsor her parents could not help noticing that her conversation, all at once, was all about carburettors and sparking plugs, how to change rotor arms and decarbonize valves.

This brief, cushioned spell of military life also gave her her first small glimpse of what life was like outside the ivory-tower atmosphere of her own upbringing, as was revealed the day her newly-appointed lady-in-waiting turned up for work without a hat on her head.

Her mother was horrified. " She must wear a hat. You must speak to her about it."

" Oh, that's old-fashioned, Mummy," replied Elizabeth.

She was wearing her A.T.S. uniform when she appeared with her parents and Winston Churchill on the palace balcony on VE Day. That night, and the next night, she and Margaret made a rare excursion outside the palace to mingle with the celebrating crowds in Trafalgar Square and Piccadilly Circus. They stood together outside the palace, adding to the public clamour of " We want the King ", and we have Margaret's own word for it that they even joined in the sport of knocking other people's hats off. Another outing with Margaret, later that year, was to the theatre, to see a play about George IV entitled *The First Gentleman*. Their escort that night was a newly-appointed equerry named Peter Townsend.

She was again on the palace balcony with her parents on VJ Day, this time in a light summery dress and wielding a newly-acquired movie camera to film the scenes around the Victoria Memorial and along the Mall. That summer, with her parents, she re-visited Balmoral for the first time since the early days of war. She was now nineteen but still inclined to dress in a somewhat juvenile fashion of pleated skirts, woollen twin-sets and boxy jackets, a rather leggy young woman with an upright carriage and a clear, carrying voice.

At Balmoral, that year, she went stalking for the first time. A shortage of clothing coupons prevented her from buying suitable clothes for the expedition and she borrowed a pair of her father's old plus-fours. Margaret thought she looked "unfeminine" in them, but Elizabeth found them extremely practical. So much so that she has continued to wear something similar, plus-fours or knickerbockers, whenever she has gone stalking over the years since.

At Buckingham Palace she no longer shared the nursery with Margaret. Instead, she had her own apartment of sitting-room, bedroom, dressing-room and bathroom overlooking the Mall. She also had her own "staff", a fact of which she was extremely proud, though it consisted at the time of only a single housemaid and a young footman.

Royal chores continued to increase. She became president of the Student Nurses' Association, the Life Saving Society and the Red Cross. Handshakes, speeches and bouquets were now part and parcel of her way of life. She starred in a film about her work—*Heir To The Throne*. The number of her public engagements shot up from eight in 1944 to thirty in 1945 and double that in 1946.

On many of those early public engagements—to a stocking factory at Baldock, a research laboratory at Wembley and the power station at Battersea—she was accompanied by the imperiously upright figure of her indefatigable grandmother, Queen Mary. She journeyed to Edinburgh with her parents for an end-of-war thanksgiving service in St Giles' Cathedral, inspected Girl Guides in Wales and toured the counties of Northern Ireland.

She was in so many ways her father's daughter, but here and there her mother's touch showed through. Given a pair of embroidered sheets in Ireland, she insisted on meeting the elderly woman who had done such fine needlework.

" Your poor eyes must ache," she sympathized with her.

On a lighter note, there were visits to the races with her father, Ascot, Epsom and Hurst Park, as well as to the bloodstock sales at Newmarket. She had been keen on racing since her early teens and, listening on the radio, had been extremely disappointed when her father's colt Big Game failed to win the 1942 wartime Derby. Now, at Ascot, she was permitted the privilege of watching the jockeys weigh in and became so caught up with the racing that she stayed on after her father had left.

On a personal level, of course, she was seeing a great deal of Philip.* With her twenty-first birthday—and a royal tour of South Africa coming up—she wanted to become engaged. But her father, though consenting to a secret, unofficial " understanding ", would not permit a formal announcement.

For the South African tour she was given an extra allotment of clothing coupons, most of which found their way to the Norman Hartnell establishment in Bruton Street. Her own fashion sense still undeveloped—indeed, she seemed to have little interest in clothes—she was content to be guided by Hartnell and her mother. The result was typically " royal " . . . pastel shades, full skirts, lavish embroidery.

The South African tour lasted four months. She saw Table Mountain and the Victoria Falls; travelled on the footplate of the famous White Train. Visiting the Free State Game Reserve, she had her first experience of flying. Her mother's influence again showed through when she inspected Basuto Girl Guides. She noticed one small group apparently being kept apart from all the rest. She asked about them and were told they were lepers. Immediately she went over to talk to them.

Back home, Britain was undergoing its toughest winter for sixty-six years, a winter rendered all the harder by coal shortage and continued food rationing. Elizabeth, reading about it in the papers, felt " guilty " at being away from it all.

---

* Those who would like more details of her courtship will find them in *The Crown And The Ring.*

She celebrated her twenty-first birthday in South Africa. Gifts —mostly diamonds—were showered upon her from all directions. There was a casket of diamonds in East London, another in Cape Town, two superb blue and white diamonds from De Beers.

From Government House on her birthday she made her memorable broadcast of dedication :

" I declare before you all that my whole life, whether it be long or short, shall be devoted to your service and the service of the great Imperial Commonwealth to which we all belong."

The speech was drafted for her by her father's Private Secretary. But the words so echoed her own sentiments that, reading it through beforehand, she was moved to tears.

Then it was back to Britain, to engagement and marriage, to an income increased from £6,000 to £15,000 and then to £30,000 a year, to her own home at Clarence House (though not for two years), her own Household as Duchess of Edinburgh. She appointed Major Martin Charteris, a former intelligence officer, as her Private Secretary and Lieutenant General Sir Frederick Browning, former chief of staff to Mountbatten, as Comptroller and Treasurer. Philip's old sidekick of his wartime sea-going days, Michael Parker, became his Private Secretary.

Her father's health, though she did not yet know it, was beginning to fail. In the autumn of 1948, as she prepared for the birth of her first child, specialists were debating whether or not the King's right leg should be amputated. Anxious not to worry her, her father would not permit her to be told until the baby was born. Then it was Philip who broke the news to her, just as, a little over three years later, he was to break the news of her father's death.

Despite his own failing health, the King did his best to limit the amount of extra work falling on his daughter's shoulders. " There will be enough for her to do later," he said.

But inevitably the burden on her increased as his health declined still further. With Philip at her side, she carried out a series of provincial tours in Britain, including another visit to Northern Ireland and a stormy crossing (which made her seasick) to the Channel Isles. She deputized for her father at the annual ceremony of Trooping the Colour, riding side-saddle on to the parade ground while he, convalescent after major surgery, watched from his carriage.

Philip resumed his naval career and she commuted back and forth to Malta to be with him as much as possible. But always there was more and more to do on behalf of her sick father. She received President Auriol of France on a state visit, helped to entertain the King and Queen of Denmark, deputized for her father on the arrival in London of the King of Norway.

She seemed almost to dash from one provincial centre to another in a growing welter of public engagements, her own and her father's. With Philip, she went over the details of their coming tour of Canada and the United States. They had planned to go by sea, but were forced to postpone their departure as the King's condition deteriorated and further surgery was necessary.

It was Philip who suggested that they should fly instead. There was immediate consternation in high places at the idea of the Heiress Presumptive flying the Atlantic despite the fact that she had been flying back and forth to Malta more or less regularly. But in the end Philip managed to talk Prime Minister Clement Attlee round. Then, as now, he was a persuasive talker.

The flight took seventeen hours and left Elizabeth, worried about her father and nervous of the tour ahead, almost exhausted. Philip, in turn, was worried about her and the tour got off to a bad start. She was sometimes stiff and unsmiling; he was grumpy. Yet she could still produce those deft human touches which are now her royal trademark.

At one hospital she visited a crippled boy had been hoping to take a photograph of her. At the last moment the flash attachment of his camera failed to function. The kid was close to tears. "Don't worry," she told him. "Get it mended and I'll come back." And she did.

Regularly she put through a telephone call to Clarence House to find out how Charles and Anne were doing in her absence. Equally regularly she called Buckingham Palace to inquire about her father. There was a seeming improvement in his condition and she was naturally overjoyed.

In Canada, over a period of five weeks, she travelled 16,000 miles and visited more than seventy places. She toured hospitals and factories, visited grain elevators and paper mills, watched an ice hockey game and the Calgary Stampede, visited McGill University and met the Dionne quins. In Ottawa, in a single day, she carried out thirteen public engagements, not counting a luncheon and a banquet. She went square dancing in a check blouse and flared skirt bought hurriedly at a convenient department store. Philip's jeans were bought just as hurriedly—and he forgot to take the price tag off! Then it was on to Washington, where she saw the Capitol and the Library of Congress, the Supreme Court and Mount Vernon, met President Truman (who called her " a fairytale princess ") and shook a staggering total of 1,600 hands during a reception at the British Embassy.

Her father was so delighted with her success that he appointed both her and Philip members of the Privy Council on their return. He was no longer so concerned that his physicians were insisting that he should again put off his own already-once-postponed tour of Australia and New Zealand. The tour would go ahead, he said, but Lilibet and Philip would go instead.

It was a dying King who journeyed to Sandringham that Christmas for the traditional family gathering. But still the inevitable boxes pursued him. It took him longer than previously to plough through their contents and his Christmas broadcast, that year, was painstakingly recorded a few words at a time. He tired easily and slept on the ground floor to ease the strain on his exhausted body.

On 31st January, having journeyed to London to wish his daughter and son-in-law godspeed at the start of their long journey to Australia and New Zealand, he stood in the open at London airport, his face haggard, his bare head whipped by a biting wind. No one who saw him that day could fail to realize that he was a desperately sick man.

But one close observer noticed something else also—the look in the King's eyes as he waved farewell to his daughter.

" It was a strange, sad look," he remembers. " Almost as though he sensed that he was seeing her for the last time."

4

Accession and Coronation

Because no one knows for certain exactly when King George VI died, no one knows exactly when his daughter, Princess Elizabeth, Duchess of Edinburgh, became Queen.

Somewhere around midnight, as 5th February 1952 became 6th February, a security man patrolling the grounds at Sandringham, where the King was staying with his wife, daughter Margaret and his two small grandchildren, Charles and Anne, heard the sound of someone fumbling with a window catch. It was assumed later that it must have been the King, opening the window of his downstairs bedroom to let in a breath of fresh air. But it is not certain.

All that is known for certain is that the King was still alive shortly after ten o'clock on 5th February as he sat listening to a news bulletin on the radio. At 7.30 the following morning when his valet, James Macdonald, went to call him as usual with his morning pot of tea, he failed to wake him.

One other thing is certain : that the dying King's last day was a happy one. He had spent it in the way he loved best, out in the open, gun in hand, shooting hares in company with his old friend and Norfolk neighbour, the late Lord Fermoy. It was a crisp cold winter's day, bright with sunshine.

Tired after the day's shooting, the King went along to his ground-floor bedroom to rest. But he was up again to say bedtime prayers with his grandchildren, as he did every evening. He had dinner with his wife and daughter, then took a stroll on the terrace. He came indoors again in time to hear the ten o'clock news and retired to bed shortly after.

In Kenya, three hours ahead of Greenwich, it was just after one o'clock in the morning. Some time between then and half-past ten that morning (Nairobi time) Princess Elizabeth became Queen Elizabeth II. She was wearing slacks and a shirt and was perched thirty feet up in the branches of a giant fig tree in the Aberdare Forest.

Her visit to the Aberdare Forest had been arranged as a break in the long trip to Australia and New Zealand she was making with Prince Philip as deputy for her father. The two of them had flown out to Nairobi and were going on from Mombasa by sea. In between, they were spending a few days in the royal hunting lodge at Sagana which had been one of their wedding gifts. They had driven over from Sagana to spend the night in the small rest house, built into the branches of the fig tree, which was the forerunner of the present Treetops.

With her movie camera, that evening of 5th February, the Princess took shots of the baboons scampering about the branches of the fig tree and filmed the elephants that came to drink at the waterhole below. But it was perhaps the Queen, though she herself did not yet know it, who was up again before dawn and again busy with her movie camera, filming a herd of rhinoceros.

After breakfast she drove back to Sagana and spent the remainder of the morning catching up with her correspondence. Around two o'clock that afternoon—11 a.m. in London—the telephone rang in the small room at the rear of the lodge which royal aides were using as a temporary office. Philip's private secretary, Michael Parker, took the call. He found himself talking to Granville Roberts, at that time a reporter with the *East African Standard*.

" There's the most awful news," Roberts told him. " The King is dead."

" Oh, no," Parker exclaimed. Then he asked, " Is it official?"

It was not—not yet. Roberts had received the news from his office, who had had it from Reuters. Martin Charteris, private secretary to the Princess,* who was with Roberts in Nyeri, took over the telephone. Authentic though the flash from Reuters undoubtedly was, he and Parker agreed that they needed something more official before informing the Princess. It came soon after in the form of a radio news flash.

---

* Now Sir Martin Charteris, the Queen's Private Secretary.

It was Parker who told Prince Philip and it was Philip who broke the news to his young wife that she was now Queen.

No one other than Philip saw her for the next hour. When they did it was clear that she had been crying.

Tragic though the news was for her, the King's death was not completely unexpected. He had been seriously ill for so long and for months past his daughter, wherever she went, had taken with her a large sealed envelope to be opened in the event of her father's death. It had gone with her to Canada the previous autumn. Now, in Kenya, she opened it. Inside was a copy of the formal declaration she would be required to make on her Accession to the Throne together with draft messages to both Houses of Parliament.

The solitary telephone line which linked the Sagana lodge with the outside world was in constant use as arrangements were made to ferry the new Queen back to London as quickly as possible. Fortunately, the aircraft in which she had flown out to Kenya was still standing by at Entebbe to fly any surplus baggage back home once she had boarded the *Gothic* and sailed from Mombasa. The problem was how to get to Entebbe. East African Airlines came to the rescue with a Dakota. Unpressurized, it was hardly the most comfortable form of royal transport, but it was all there was. Quickly the Queen's maid, Margaret Macdonald, and Philip's valet, John Dean, packed the royal belongings. By sunset the Queen was at Nanyuki, where the Dakota was waiting. By midnight she was in Entebbe and switching from the Dakota to the Argonaut for the long flight back to London.

She was still wearing one of the light summery dresses she had taken with her to Sagana. The rest of her wardrobe, including the mourning outfit which is always included in royal luggage, was already aboard the *Gothic* and there had been no time to get it back. However, a refuelling touchdown at El Adem, a desert staging post near Tobruk, enabled the Queen to send a telegram to Clarence House, as a result of which a car drew alongside her aircraft as soon as it touched down in London. Suitcases were quickly transferred from car to plane. As the aircraft taxied slowly round to the official reception point, the Queen changed quickly out of her holiday clothes and into mourning.

Despite her long years of training, it was with difficulty that she managed to keep her emotions in check. At first, her face strained, she could not bring herself to reply to those who greeted her. Finally she managed a few words. " This is a very tragic homecoming." She was not alone in her emotions. Winston Churchill, the prime minister, had tears running unashamedly down his cheeks.

At Clarence House, Queen Mary was waiting to greet the grand-daughter she had coached so painstakingly towards this moment of monarchy. As a child, it had been the Queen, as Princess Elizabeth, who had curtsied to her grandmother as Queen. Now their roles were reversed and it was Queen Mary, as regally dutiful as ever at eighty-four, who curtsied to her grand-daughter.

" I wanted your old Granny to be the first of your subjects to kiss your hand, Your Majesty," she said.

But she did not, it would seem, entirely approve of the clothes her grand-daughter was wearing. " Much too short for mourning," she is said to have commented.

Also awaiting the Queen at Clarence House was the first of her boxes, though the name lettered in gold on the leather-covered lid was still that of " The King." There had not yet been time to change it.

From Clarence House the Queen put through a telephone call to her mother at Sandringham. It was the best she could do. In an ordinary family, on the death of her father, a daughter would have rushed straight to her mother's side. It is one of the penalties of being royal that duty must always come first. And first, before going to see her mother, the daughter, because she was Queen, must see her Lord Chamberlain and the Duke of Norfolk, Earl Marshal of England, and command arrangements for the dead King's funeral. She must also make her Declaration of Accession, as she did the following morning at St James's Palace.

Her grandfather, King George V, after his Declaration of Accession, had noted in his diary: " The most trying ordeal I have ever had to go through." He was a man in his forties at the time and, while he may have respected his dead father, can hardly have been said to have loved him. The Queen was a young woman in her twenties and no daughter can have loved her father more.

Her face was pale and her eyes clouded as she read the passage in the Declaration referring to " my revered and beloved father."

But her strong will and long years of training stood her in good stead.

Her voice level, she went on : " My heart is too full for me to say more to you today than that I shall always work, as my father did throughout his reign, to uphold the Constitutional Government and to advance the happiness and prosperity of my peoples . . .

" I know that in my resolve to follow his shining example of service and devotion, I shall be inspired by the loyalty and affection of those whose Queen I have been called to be . . .

" I pray that God will help me to discharge worthily this heavy task which has been laid upon me so early in life."

When it was all over, her husband and her uncle, the Duke of Gloucester, escorted her back to Clarence House. From a window looking out on to the courtyard of St James's Palace she watched the historic ceremony of proclamation. That done, she left for Sandringham.

She was asked if she would like to see her father's body. She declined, preferring to remember him as he was in life. That night, after dark, the coffin was wheeled across the park to the tiny church of St Mary Magdalene. The King's piper who was now the Queen's piper led the small procession. Behind the coffin came the Queen, the Queen Mother, Prince Philip, Princess Margaret and a small handful of loyal servants, like James Macdonald, who had been closest to the King. On the coffin, as it lay in the church, was a single all-white wreath. On the card, in the Queen's handwriting, were the words : " To darling Papa from your sorrowing Lilibet."

In a way it was perhaps fortunate for the Queen that the months immediately following her father's death were to be among the busiest of her life. There was little time to look back, to dwell on the past, to grieve. Even the King's funeral—at St George's Chapel, Windsor, on 15th February—involved his daughter in receiving monarchs and presidents, Commonwealth prime ministers and high commissioners. There was the Prime Minister to be seen weekly, other ministers to be received in Audience, new appointments to be made or approved. In a single day, not long after her accession, the new Queen received the Sheriffs of the City of London, the chairman of the London County Council, the Lord Provost of Edinburgh, the governor of the Bank of England, the presidents of the Royal Academy and the Royal Society, and Britain's new ambassador to Turkey. There were the hardy perennials of the royal round to be dealt with. She distributed the Royal Maundy and invested those named in her father's last honours list. And always there were the inevitable boxes.

The question of her name—" My own, of course; what else?"—had been dealt with while still in Kenya. There remained the question of a surname. On Churchill's advice, to preserve the continuity of monarchy, she reverted to her maiden name of Windsor.

There was also the question of where to live. Left entirely to her own devices, the Queen would have much preferred to stay on at Clarence House, using Buckingham Palace simply as the working headquarters of monarchy. Winston Churchill shook his head. It would never do, he advised. The Monarch must live at the Palace. So during the six weeks of spring when Monarch and Court are traditionally resident at Windsor, removal men were busy shifting the contents of Clarence House along the Mall to the palace.

The move was complicated by the fact that the Queen Mother was moving into Clarence House, but could hardly do so until her daughter had moved out, while the Queen, in turn, could not move into the royal apartment at the palace until her mother had vacated it. As a stop-gap measure she moved first into the Belgian Suite at the rear. However, the Belgian Suite could not accommodate the children as well and, to help out, Princess Margaret surrendered the second floor suite which she and her sister had had as a nursery in childhood so that it could again become a nursery for her sister's children.

The Queen was anxious that her children should not feel as unsettled as she herself had done when she moved from Piccadilly to Buckingham Palace in childhood. That they did not was due in no small measure to the motherly skill of her arrangements. When they drove back to the palace instead of Clarence House after the six weeks at Windsor, they found their new nursery looking almost exactly like the old one at Clarence House, the same chintz curtains at the windows, the same table at meal-times, the same glass-fronted cabinet holding the same familiar books and toys.

For the Queen, every day brought the same procession of private secretaries and other royal aides. Twice a day, and sometimes more often than that, a horse-drawn brougham (to be replaced some years later by a car) clip-clopped into the palace yard with yet another of the inevitable boxes. There was a daily summary of proceedings in Parliament to be digested and similar summaries of Commonwealth affairs. There were photographs to be signed and dispatched to British embassies and elsewhere. Of course, the Queen did not do the packing and dispatching herself. But she did do the signing. Someone suggested having a rubber-stamp made of her *Elizabeth R* signature. She declined. She would sign each photograph personally, she said; a facsimile signature would not be the same.

There were portraits to be sat for and here the Queen could and did reduce her workload. More than one royal portrait of the time was completed from a dressmaker's dummy draped in the Queen's clothes.

Among the several paintings executed at this time was one which the Queen commissioned for herself. Her father, when she was young, had had a family group painted of himself, his wife and their two daughters. The Queen wanted a matching group of herself, Philip and their two children. But even for this she could spare time to pose for only the features. Her dresser, Margaret Macdonald, acted as stand-in for the rest of the painting.

A rare visitor to the palace that first year of monarchy was the Duke of Windsor, still smarting from the fact that his wife did not have the style of Her Royal Highness, though this had been freely accorded to the Queen's two other aunts by marriage, the Duchess of Gloucester and the widowed Princess Marina. The Queen's father, while granting his brother the style of Royal Highness at the time of the Abdication, had made a point of excluding the Duchess of Windsor and any children that might result from the marriage. So hurt and incensed was Windsor by this that he refused to return to Britain with his wife until this (as he thought) slight on her was removed. In private, following a luncheon party held to celebrate the Queen and Prince Philip's fifth wedding anniversary, this delicate subject was now raised again. But the Queen, just as she had so far insisted on doing things exactly as her father had always done them, was equally not prepared to do something he had specifically refrained from doing.

In her role as Monarch the Queen shirked nothing and would take no short cuts. Over a period of five months in that first year of monarchy she carried out 140 official engagements and it hardly surprised those close to her when she was taken ill just before one investiture. Margaret offered to deputize for her, but she would not have it. She was the Queen and must do it herself, she insisted. Duty done, she retired to her bedroom and took to her bed. Others had already seen that she was in danger of over-working herself. An article in *The Lancet* suggested that she was doing too much and would injure her health if she did not ease up. And the Select Committee appointed to agree a new Civil List commented upon the " formidable " burden she was required to bear and pointed out that the " increasing facilities of air travel . . . are certain to mean a considerable extension in the demands made upon Her Majesty ".

But if the Queen was perhaps trying to do too much, Philip had too little to occupy his time. He saw, as the Queen Mother had seen at the time of the Abdication, that things were going to be very different in the future and, for a time, he was consider-ably depressed. He had given up his naval career in order to help his wife and now she no longer needed his help. Or, though she may have needed it, was constitutionally—in many things—not permitted to have it. He could help her with selecting designs for new postal stamps and the new coinage, and this he did. He could hardly help with the design for the Queen's coronation gown. Queen Mary took over, marching her grand-daughter along to study the gown Queen Victoria had worn at her coronation.

But the grand-daughter was developing a mind of her own and preferred something different. Queen Victoria, as she pointed out, " was unmarried at the time of her coronation " while she herself was a married woman. Instead of an all-white gown such as Victoria had worn, she suggested to Norman Hartnell, who designed it, that hers should be embroidered with the symbols of all the countries of which she was Queen.

By Christmas the gown was ready for its first fitting. The Queen was at Sandringham and Hartnell went there with his assistants. " It's glorious," the Queen exclaimed as she tried on

E

the weighty creation with its embroidered designs in pearls, crystal and *diamanté*.

By the time she returned from Sandringham preparations for the coronation were in full swing. The long robe of royal purple which she would wear for part of the coronation ceremony was brought out of storage for her to try on. Out of storage too came the state liveries for royal servants, unworn since pre-war days. Stored in metal boxes in the palace basement, they had survived the passage of the years well . . . except for the silk stockings. The moths had been at these and they had to be replaced. In the royal mews the state coach was being refurbished with new panelling. Its wheels were re-shod with rubber instead of iron to make for a smoother ride and battery operated rose-tinted lights were installed so that the Queen could be better seen as she journeyed to and from Westminster Abbey.

As the days and weeks passed towards the coronation, the Queen was perhaps as excited as she has ever been in her life. But excitement was also tinged with sadness at the illness of her grandmother, Queen Mary. Weekly the Queen went to see her grandmother at Marlborough House. Each time she found her a little worse. But to the end, for Queen Mary, duty came first. Whatever happened to her, she told those close to her, the coronation must go ahead. On 24th March, a bare ten weeks before the ceremony to which she had looked forward almost as eagerly as her grand-daughter, the old lady died.

Her dying wish, it is said, was to see her grand-daughter with her crown on her head. According to legend, she did. Legend has it that, with Churchill's connivance, what is known as the Crown of St Edward (though it was actually made for the coronation of Charles II) was taken secretly to Marlborough House. Secretly the Queen went there too and, in the bedroom where Queen Mary lay dying, she put it on.

We cannot vouch for the story. With Churchill and Queen Mary both dead, perhaps only the Queen knows whether it is true or not. The nearest we have managed to get to confirming it was in conversation with a former royal servant who knew both the Queen and Queen Mary at the time of which we are writing. He could not help us directly. He had heard the story himself, but had no personal knowledge of whether it was true or not.

But this much he did say: " It could very well be true. It's the sort of thing that's in line with both their characters."

Anxious to minimize the strain on the Queen as much as possible, members of the Coronation Committee came up with various suggestions for abridging things. One suggestion was that the processional route should be shortened.

Far from agreeing, the Queen asked for the route to be extended, with special places allotted to schoolchildren.

She intervened also in the controversy as to whether or not the ceremony should be televised. The Coronation Committee's initial decision was against such an innovation which, it was thought, could only increase the strain on the Queen. Such a storm of public protest resulted from the news that the Committee decided upon a compromise. The procession in Westminster Abbey could be televised, but not the actual coronation ceremony. It was at this stage that the Queen herself intervened. She wanted all her subjects to share the occasion with her as fully as possible, she said.

But as so often, the new decision to televise brought yet another problem—the question of what make-up the Queen should wear to look equally good on television, under the yellow lights of the Abbey and in the state coach with its rose-tinted lighting. Trial and error eventually produced a satisfactory solution.

The Queen went to Westminster Abbey for a run through. In this, as in everything else, she was nothing if not thorough. When Philip, who was also taking part, appeared to be treating things too lightly, she called him back. " Please do it again," she said. " Properly this time."

There were other rehearsals in the privacy of her palace home. In the Picture Gallery chairs were set out to represent the state coach. With her maids-of-honour in attendance and a footman standing in for Prince Philip, the Queen, a sheet pinned to her shoulders to represent her robe, practised getting in and out of the make-believe coach.

As a thank-you gesture to those who worked for her, the Queen invited servants from her various residences—Buckingham Palace and Windsor Castle, Balmoral Castle and Sandringham—to be the first to see her on Coronation Day. With their wives and children, relatives and friends, they crowded the Grand Hall and a mass gasp went up as the Queen appeared at the head of the marble steps, a radiantly smiling figure in her coronation gown, a pearl and diamond diadem on her head, her robe of crimson velvet draped over one arm.

Slowly she descended the steps, walking between the Yeomen of the Guard in their Tudor tunics and ruffs and so out to the waiting coach.

There is a legend that wherever the Queen goes the clouds disperse and the sun shines. " The Queen's weather " it is called. Coronation Day proved it to be the purest fiction. As the Queen climbed into the state coach, sheltered by the portico of the Grand Entrance, is was already drizzling with rain. Later the drizzle became a downpour.

The signal was given and the procession moved off, the four-ton coach swaying on its leather braces like a ship at sea. As it emerged through the palace gates the murmur of the dense crowd along the Mall became a sudden thunderclap of sound. Footmen and postillions old enough to remember the coronation of the Queen's father had prepared for it by stuffing their ears with cottonwool. As a result, one at least failed to hear shouted instructions from Prince Philip at one stage of the return trip.

As we write this, it is nearly twenty-three years since the Coronation—which did not take place until sixteen months after the actual accession—and inevitably time blurs the picture. But some things remain vivid and clear-cut, etched indelibly on the videotape of memory : the triumphant shout of *Vivat Regina* from the boys of Westminster school as the thirty-ninth monarch to be crowned there is first glimpsed in the abbey; the Queen Mother curtsying to her daughter; the boy Charles kneeling on his stool to obtain a better view of the proceedings and the Queen's eyes flickering mother-like towards him; the Queen kneeling as she affirms " The things which I have herebefore promised I will perform and keep, so help me God "; the trumpets exulting and the mass shout of " God Save The Queen " as the overlarge crown of St. Edward made originally to fit over the wig of Charles II, is placed on her head; her head tilting momentarily backwards under its weight, her face unsmiling and remote; Prince Philip swearing allegiance to the monarch who was also his wife. And who among those who saw it—at first-hand or on television—will ever forget the giant figure of Queen Salote of Tonga grinning her way through the rain outside the abbey, a bit player stealing the limelight briefly from the star of the show.

The Queen's grandfather, King George V, writing about his own coronation, described it as " a terrible ordeal." If the Queen felt the same, it showed only momentarily here and there, and she emerged from the abbey after her three-hour endurance test looking as tireless and self-composed as when she had entered.

Then came the procession back to the palace through rain-swept streets and cheering crowds, the crimson robe in which she had arrived at the abbey now replaced by one of monarchical purple, on her head not the massive Crown of St. Edward, but the lighter Imperial State Crown. In one hand, as she rode through the streets of London, she held the Sovereign's Sceptre; on the palm of the other was balanced the Sovereign's Orb. Or so it seemed to those watching. In fact, the weight of the orb was taken by a cunningly concealed ledge while the sceptre was slotted into hidden brackets. Even for coronations, things are not always what they seem.

There was a brief moment when the Queen, climbing back into the state coach, wondered if its ship-like sway might bring on an attack of travel sickness during the long roundabout route of the return trip. It did not and back at the palace she went straight out on to the balcony to acknowledge the cheers of the crowd. Again and again they demanded her presence on the balcony and again and again she was happy to respond, smiling now that the actual ordeal of ceremony was over, looking as fresh and radiant throughout the evening as she had done when she first descended the Grand Staircase on her way to the abbey. Ignoring so small a matter as sex, the crowd, at one stage of the proceedings, hailed her in song : " For *she's* a jolly good fellow."

In a broadcast from the palace that evening the Queen said, " I have in sincerity pledged myself to your service as many of you are pledged to mine. Throughout all my life, and with all my heart, I shall strive to be worthy of your trust. In this resolve I have my husband to support me. He shares all my ideals and all my affection for you. Then, although my experience is so short and my task so new, I have in my parents and grandparents an example I can follow with certainty of confidence."

The seven hours of television transmission that day were seen on nearly three million sets in Britain, France, Germany and the Netherlands—a large number for those pre-satellite days—as well as by audiences in theatres and cinemas in London, Manchester, Leeds and Doncaster. It was around midnight when the newly-crowned Queen appeared on the palace balcony to take her last " call " and the curtain was finally rung down on what Churchill, with his graphic gift for the right phrase, called " A day the oldest are proud to have lived to see and the youngest will remember all their lives."

5

The Years of Monarchy

Her fiftieth birthday behind her, her silver wedding anniversary fading into memory, the mother of four children (two of whom are older than she was herself when she succeeded to the throne), it is inevitable that the passage of years should have changed the Queen as it changes all of us.

She is no longer the " fairytale princess "—the words were President Truman's—who became Queen in 1952, and that is as it should be. Her mother, when she was not much older than the Queen is now, commissioned a set of birthday portraits from a famous photographer. The proofs, when she saw them, showed signs of some slight re-touching.

" They're very nice, of course," said the Queen Mother, " but they're not quite me, are they? I don't want people thinking I have come through my years on earth completely unscathed."

The Queen, in the same sort of situation today, would perhaps say the same. In a fast-changing world, her years of monarchy have not been easy ones. There have been problems from time to time in her personal life too and in that shadowy, ill-defined area where woman and monarch meet.

The first big problem, one which was to involve her on both personal and public levels, was already simmering behind the scenes at the time of her coronation. It was the problem of Princess Margaret's attachment to Peter Townsend, the wartime fighter ace who went to Buckingham Palace as equerry to the late King originally on a three-month basis and, because the King took a liking to him, was to stay on until the headline-making gossip of coronation year saw him hurriedly despatched to Brussels as British air attaché.

Margaret, at the time, was a young woman of twenty-three,

away with her mother on a royal visit to Southern Rhodesia. Townsend should have gone with them to mastermind the trip. But at the last moment the late Lord Plunket went instead and Townsend stayed behind to accompany the Queen on her visit to Northern Ireland. By the time Margaret got back he was in Brussels. It was to be more than two years before they saw each other again.

For the Queen, these early years of monarchy were both busy and exciting. Hardly was the Coronation over than she was plunged into arrangements for her six-month round-the-world tour.* There were, in addition, the visit to Northern Ireland, similar visits to Wales and Scotland, investitures and Privy Councils, receptions, reviews and inspections. She returned from her world tour to the renewed pressure of piled-up engagements. Over the next eighteen months she acted as host to the King of Sweden, the Presidents of France and Portugal, Prince Bernhardt of the Netherlands, King Feisal of Iraq, King Hussein of Jordan, the Shah of Persia and the Emperor of Ethiopia. She crossed the North Sea in the new royal yacht *Britannia* to visit Norway, the first of many similar state visits. But there was time also to watch her favourite racehorse Aureole make her the year's most successful owner.

She had been disappointed when Aureole had failed to win the Derby of Coronation year.

" If I had to be beaten, I'm glad it was by you," she said graciously to Gordon Richards whose mount, Pinza, beat Aureole into second place.

But now, in 1954, Aureole was to bring her victory after victory, the Coronation Cup, the Hardwicke Stakes, the King George VI and Queen Elizabeth Stakes. Watching this last race, the Queen was so excited that she hopped up and down in the royal box, shouting encouragement to royal horse and jockey. " We've done it. We've done it," she exclaimed, clapping her hands with delight as Aureole passed the winning post just ahead of Madame Volterra's Vamos.

If some critics muttered that she spent too much time at the races in those early years of monarchy, neither royal duty nor family life were in any way neglected. Cleverly dovetailing her

* Chapter 6.

twin roles of monarch and mother, the Queen would have her children with her each morning for the first half-hour of the day. And each evening after work she would hurry upstairs to the palace nursery, tie a plastic apron on over her dress to bath them, play with them and put them to bed. Permitting nothing to interfere with this small family interlude, she even arranged for her regular Tuesday evening session with the Prime Minister to be put back until after the children's bedtime. Often Philip would join her in the nursery of an evening, playing with the children in their bath and reading them a bedtime story before they settled down for the night.

Busy as she was in so many different directions, the Queen saw her first year or two of monarchy slip by at almost breakneck speed, and in no time at all, it seemed, she was arranging for Charles to start lessons. She engaged a governess, Katharine Peebles, to take him through much the same sort of light curriculum she herself had experienced in childhood. She also arranged for him to have the same sort of outings on which Queen Mary had once taken her, trips to the Zoo and the Tower of London, visits to museums and art galleries. She hoped, she said, that he would be permitted to enjoy such outings " in the same way as other children can, without the embarrassment of constant publicity ".

In this, she was to be disappointed. With all the excitement of a new reign and a new young Queen, the promise of a bright new Elizabethan age (which sadly failed to materialize), public interest in the Royal Family proved greater than ever and newspapers and magazines, eager to boost their circulations, were quick to cater for it. During these early years of monarchy the Queen and her family were to be subject to the same sort of sometimes unhealthy attention which movie stars had attracted earlier and pop stars were to attract later. Those who advised the Queen did not always know how to cope with this new situation and the Queen herself seemed sometimes unaware of the possible consequences of her own actions.

In arranging to act as saleswoman at a sale-of-work in aid of Crathie parish church during her annual stay at Balmoral, for instance, she would seem to have completely overlooked the frenzied adulation to which she and her family were subject. The sale-of-work attracted such crowds that the final scene was

certainly chaotic and not far short of a riot. Children were hurt
in the crush, clothes torn and the rear of one marquee ripped
open by those eager to buy from the Queen herself. In all the
excitement someone even sold the Queen's coat which she had
removed because she was too hot. Her favourite diamond brooch
was pinned to the coat. Fortunately, she noticed the disappear-
ance of the coat in time and coat and brooch were safely retrieved
for her.

That was in 1955, the year in which the new Annigoni
portrait of the Queen was unveiled at the Royal Academy, when
she drove to Downing Street to dine with Churchill on his retirement as Prime Minister and when she unveiled a memorial in
the Mall to her dead father. She was clearly speaking from the
heart when she said,

"Much was asked of my father in personal sacrifice and
endeavour, often in the face of illness. His courage in overcoming
it endeared him to everybody. He shirked no task, however
difficult, and to the end never faltered in his duty to his peoples."

It was also the year of Princess Margaret's twenty-fifth birthday. At twenty-five, she was now free of the restrictions of
George III's Royal Marriage Act under which she had previously
needed the consent of "the Sovereign in Council" before she
could marry and that autumn Peter Townsend returned to
London. There was a warm reunion between the two at Clarence
House, where Margaret was now living with her mother, and
they spent subsequent weekends together at the country homes
of relatives and friends as the Princess sought to resolve her
romantic dilemma.

The so-called "Permissive Age" was not yet upon us and out-
looks and attitudes were stricter. The Duke of Windsor had been
compelled to abdicate in order to marry an American divorcee.
Nor could the Queen's sister marry a divorced man, however
innocent, without compromising the Queen's position as head of
the Church of England, and the Queen presumably said as much
during the weekend Margaret spent with her and Philip at
Windsor. Certainly when the three of them emerged from the
Queen's sitting-room at bedtime the Queen looked strained,
Philip grim and Margaret's eyes were evidence that she had been
crying. A few days later she issued her touching statement of
renunciation.

Those who may have thought that the Queen's youth would blow like a fresh breeze through the musty confines of Buckingham Palace, bringing a new, more informal relationship between monarch and people, were beginning to find their hopes dashed. With the Queen still relying to a large extent on those who had advised her father before her, there were few changes in the traditionally stereotyped order of things. True, the old-style levees of previous reigns were not to be resumed and the presentation of delicate debs was to end in another year or so. In place of these things, the Queen instituted the series of informal luncheons with guests drawn from a wide cross-section of public life which are still held several times a year. But that was all. Hardly a palace revolution!

If adulation of the Monarch was still excessive, there was also growing criticism. The Queen could perhaps ignore those who sniped at her deer stalking, who criticized the repetitiveness of her Christmas broadcast and condemned her for not sending Charles to school, but rumours of a supposed rift between her and Philip were headlines of another order.

Philip was away on his 1956-7 Antarctic trip when the storm broke and his prolonged absence served to add fuel to the fires of rumour and gossip. Michael Parker was with him on the trip and it was in fact Parker's marriage which was heading for the rocks. But rumour, as so often, got things twisted and in the newspapers it was Philip, not Parker, who was heading, if not for the divorce court, certainly for a showdown with his royal wife and the Government. It ended finally in perhaps the only way it could, with Parker's resignation.

Even this was misinterpreted. The Queen, far from demanding his resignation, cabled the royal yacht urging him to reconsider. Philip, on the spot, equally tried to talk him out of it. But Parker's mind was made up. He wanted no further gossip on his account to tarnish the image of the couple he had served loyally for so long. When *Britannia* docked at Gibraltar he packed his things and flew back to London alone. It was perhaps a tactical error which did nothing to check the rumours and headlines. Better perhaps if Philip had flown home. As it was, it led to a further newspaper story that Philip was sulking because Parker had been forced to resign. That story was as wide of the mark as all those that had gone before. There never was a " royal rift," as the Queen and her husband proved by their subsequent and obviously happy reunion in Portugal.

Nevertheless, the Queen was deeply hurt for a time. "How can they say such terrible things about us?" she asked one day when confronted by particularly glaring headlines.

Her life, at this time, was crammed with state visits. Before Portugal she had been to Sweden. After, she went to France, Denmark, the Netherlands. At home there was a renewed spate of criticisms. As with some of Willie Hamilton's more recent attacks, it was less what the critics said than the manner in which they said it that made for controversy. There were perhaps some valuable truths in an article by the then Lord Altrincham in the *National & English Review*, but these were largely overlooked in the excitement aroused by some of his more high-flown phrasing. The Queen's voice, he wrote, was " a pain in the neck," her personality that of " a priggish schoolgirl " and her friends and aides all of " the tweedy sort."

The same was true of an article by Malcolm Muggeridge in the *Saturday Evening Post* which greeted the Queen on a visit to Canada and the United States which she sandwiched between her state visits to Denmark and the Netherlands. Muggeridge's article equally contained some valuable truths, but few people in Britain had an opportunity to read them. Instead, they were treated to a rehashed summary of his more colourful adjectives and phraseology. The Royal Family was " a kind of royal soap opera," monarchy " a sort of ersatz religion " and royal aides were " quite exceptionally incompetent."

Even so, both outbursts were fairly mild compared with Willie Hamilton's more recent criticisms and would arouse little excitement today. But at the time it was as though the writers were both guilty of attempted assassination. " I would like to see the man hanged, drawn and quartered," wrote the Duke of Argyll of Altrincham. Altrincham was in fact set about in the street by an over-enthusiastic loyalist and Muggeridge was spat upon.

That the Queen was beginning, however slowly, to move more with the times was demonstrated during her visit to Canada, where she chalked up two " firsts "—her first press conference and her first telecast. The press conference was very much in the American style with few holds barred. Among other things, the

Queen was asked if she would let her mother go to Canada as Governor-General.

" Oh, no," she replied, smiling. " We couldn't possibly spare her."

Approached previously by the B.B.C. to be televised when delivering her Christmas message, she had declined. But in Canada she took her first hesitant step into the new medium. There had been a dummy run at Buckingham Palace before she left for Canada. It was a flop. But she was now obstinately determined to go through with what she regarded as a fresh aspect of royal duty.

In Canada, for another run-through, she nudged her shoes off in an attempt to relax. She still looked—and doubtless felt— terrified as she waited for the red light to come on. Then a cryptic message was relayed to her from Philip, who had earlier undergone his own first ordeal by television.

" Tell the Queen to remember the wailing and gnashing of teeth."

If no one else understood, the Queen obviously did. She smiled for the first time. The red light went on and her telecast became a complete success.

But there was no smile when, moving on from Canada to the United States, she was shown up to her hotel apartment in New York. In the lobby of the apartment was a plaque listing those who had stayed there before her, among them T.R.H. (presumably standing for Their Royal Highnesses) the Duke and Duchess of Windsor.

As explained earlier,* the Queen's father, while granting his abdicating brother the style of Royal Highness, had excluded the woman he proposed to marry. Yet here in New York the Duchess had apparently been accorded a royal status she did not possess. The Queen was not pleased and it showed.

Back home, delighted with the outcome of her television appearance in Canada, she agreed to be televised at Christmas. When the time came, however, nerves again affected her to such an extent that she left the lunch table with her Christmas meal only half eaten. But, again, the actual telecast was voted a complete success.

* Chapter 4.

Among other things, the article in the *National & English Review* had advocated that Prince Charles should be sent to a state school to mix with "children who will one day be bus-drivers, dockers and engineers—not merely with future land-owners and stockbrokers." At the time the article was published the Queen's decision as to her son's education had, in fact, already been taken. In making it, she was influenced by her husband, who thought that the time had come when the boy needed something sterner than the molly-coddling of the royal nursery. So off Charles went to school, though not to a state school as advocated by Altrincham. Instead, he went first to a day school in London and then to his father's old boarding school, Cheam.

Until now, although completely ignoring well-intentioned advice that she should take things more easily the Queen's health had been remarkably good. But following her visit to Canada and the United States came a prolonged bout of ill-health. It started as a succession of colds, some of them bad enough to compel her to cancel her engagements and take to her bed. That December she was forced to call off a weekend visit to Philip's relatives, the Brabournes. In January she was again in bed for a few days. She managed her state visit to the Netherlands in March, but the following month found her so ill that she cancelled visits to the Cup Final at Wembley and the Ascot horse show.

In June, on a day even wetter than that of her Coronation, against Prince Philip's advice, she insisted on the annual Birthday Parade being held as usual. With no coach to protect her—she rode side-saddle on horseback—she got soaked through and again ended up in bed. The following month she was again taken ill while touring Scotland, and this time she was too ill to argue when Philip insisted on her returning to Buckingham Palace while he went to Carlisle on his own. At the palace she was examined by physicians, X-rayed and ordered to go to bed and stay there. Under treatment, her cold cleared up, but the basic sinus condition remained and was to require an operation carried out under local anaesthetic.

In bed before and after the operation, she continued to deal with the contents of her boxes as usual. But public engagements were necessarily cancelled, among them a tour of Wales and a visit to the Commonwealth Games in Cardiff. Philip went to

Cardiff alone, taking with him a package which was to remain a close-kept secret until the final day of the Games. It contained a recording the Queen had made announcing the creation of her son, Charles, as Prince of Wales.

" When he is grown up," the Queen's voice said over the public address system, " I will present him to you at Caernarvon."

For the Queen, public engagements of whatever sort were no longer the novelties they had once been and it would perhaps have been excusable if she had been content to perform them in no more than routine fashion. She did not, and often there was the extra, essentially human touch. A planned tour of Essex brought a request from an old lady. She was one hundred and five, she wrote, and wanted more than anything to meet the Queen. Readily agreeing, the Queen sent word back that the old lady was on no account to leave her car. The Queen would leave hers and go over to speak to her.

Philip, busy building up his own list of public appointments and engagements, embarked on another of his long solo tours, this time to the islands of the Pacific and Far East. He was gone several months and it was April when he got back. Little more than six weeks later, just ahead of another visit to Canada and the United States, the Queen, at the age of thirty-three, happily realized that she was expecting another child.

Her third child, Andrew, was born at the palace the following February. This time it was Prince Philip, not a royal page, who called out excitedly " It's a boy," though he did not go quite so far as to announce it to the crowds waiting for news outside the palace.

Overjoyed as she was by the new baby, the Queen was also happy in the knowledge that her sister, Princess Margaret, was soon to be married, though it was to be another seven days before an official announcement issued by the Queen Mother from Clarence House let the public into the secret. " Who is he?" most people were inclined to ask when they first heard the name of Antony Armstrong-Jones.

He was—and is, as everyone now knows—a photographer of no small ability. Margaret and he first met at a society wedding in Norfolk. She was one of the wedding guests; he took the pictures. But it was not for another two years, when they met again at a party at which they were both guests, that they really began to get to know each other. Tony told Margaret about the photographic blow-ups he had created as sets for a new revue. Margaret said she would like to see the show when she got back from Sandringham. Unfortunately, it did not run that long. " A bit of a flop," Tony conceded, ruefully. Instead, they went to see the American musical, *West Side Story*.

The Townsend episode had taught Margaret an important lesson and her new romance was conducted with all the secrecy of an espionage operation. Tony, arriving to see her at Royal Lodge, would carefully cart all his equipment in with him so that it seemed he was there simply to take photographs. Sometimes he did, including the one which was issued to mark Margaret's twenty-ninth birthday. In his guise of photographer, he also visited Balmoral and was a guest at Sandringham the Christmas before Andrew was born. Even royal servants, normally the first to gossip, suspected nothing; to them he was merely " that photographer chap." The two of them went to the theatre together, carefully booking seats in other people's names and there were romantic *tête-à-têtes* at a Thames-side cottage lent by one of Tony's friends. There were similar unpublicized weekends at the country homes of other friends and secret visits by Margaret to Tony's studio-apartment in London's Pimlico Road.

Prince Philip gave the bride away when they were married at Westminster Abbey in May 1960. Princess Anne, now nearly ten, was chief bridesmaid. Despite the fact that television relayed the occasion into countless homes, Buckingham Palace insisted on labelling it " private ". Tony's charwoman and one of his former models, Jackie Chan, were among the wedding guests. So was the Queen, who also lent the couple her royal yacht for their honeymoon. The Duke of Windsor was invited, but piqued by the fact that his wife was still not a Royal Highness, did not attend. Nor, for the same reason, did he accept an invitation when the Queen's cousin, the Duke of Kent, married Katharine Worsley the following June.

Perhaps coincidentally, perhaps deliberately, the pace of public life slackened for the Queen in the weeks immediately following Andrew's birth. There was a state visit by General de Gaulle, but little else of moment. She made use of her free time to plan the remodelling of the Queen's Tower at Windsor, converting it into a more comfortable weekend apartment. For days on end, her room at the palace looked more like an interior decorator's studio than the focal point of monarchy as, with Philip's help, she selected paints, wallpapers and fabrics. Unable to find a suitable paper for one room in any of the books, she even drove to a do-it-yourself shop in Chelsea for an on-the-spot purchase of six rolls of wallpaper.

To Charles and Anne, such informal shopping expeditions and similar outings are now commonplace. For the Queen, they have always been rare. She enjoys them all the more for that and was particularly delighted, spending a weekend with her old friends, the Nevills, in Sussex, when she found herself actually queuing for seats at a Brighton theatre.

There was also, around this time, a visit to the Haymarket Theatre in London. The royal party had booked seats 3–8 in row G of the stalls, but inadvertently sat in seats 1–6. As a result, an embarrassed usherette found herself asking Philip if his party would mind moving along when the actual bookers of seats 1 and 2 arrived a few minutes later.

Mindful of the harassment her two older children had suffered —and, indeed, were still suffering—the Queen determined that nothing of this sort should beset her youngest. Perhaps she went too far to the other extreme. With few photographs issued of the new baby, little material made available to article writers, it was perhaps inevitable that rumours should start up that there was something wrong with the child. Such rumours about royal children are nothing new, of course. Margaret, as a child, was rumoured to be a deaf mute. Charles was once said to have a club foot. Now it was Andrew's turn. However, such rumours were speedily dispelled in the summer of 1961 when the Queen, following the Birthday Parade, appeared on the palace balcony with her sixteen-months-old son obviously sound in wind and limb.

The late President Kennedy and his wife Jackie were in London that year and the Queen gave a dinner in their honour. Earlier there had been a visit from ex-President Eisenhower. He and the Queen had lunch together and, like any other proud mother, the Queen could not resist bringing Andrew down from the nursery. " A fine little boy," Ike called him.

The cycle of family life was constantly repeating itself. Anne was now a Girl Guide as her mother had been before her. Like

F

her mother before her, she also took part in an amateur production of *Cinderella*. But she was not the Prince, as her mother had been. Instead, she took Aunt Margo's old role of Cinderella. Charles too enjoyed his first taste of acting in a school play at Cheam, taking the part of the ancestor who became King Richard III. The experiment of sending him to school was beginning to show signs of working out well. Following a further appeal from his royal mother, newspaper editors had finally agreed to call off their photographers and reporters and let him get on with the task of being an ordinary schoolboy.

February 1962 marked the tenth anniversary of the Queen's accession. Of those ten years, she had spent more than a year abroad, travelling 140,000 miles in visiting twenty-one Commonwealth and thirteen other countries, some of them more than once. At home, she had visited 210 different cities and towns, received 2,336 people in Audience, held 150 Privy Council meetings and ninety-five investitures. There was a lot more still to come.

That summer it was time for Charles to move on to another of his father's old schools, Gordonstoun. Philip flew him there and took advantage of the opportunity to revisit some of the scenes of his boyhood. Another year and the Queen was interrupting her annual stay at Balmoral to travel south and deliver Anne into the hands of the headmistress of Benenden. It was the Queen's own idea—not Philip's—that Anne should go to boarding school. Indeed, it was an idea she had had at the back of her mind since her 1957 state visit to Denmark when, impressed by the three young daughters of King Frederick, she learnt that they went to ordinary schools.

That year of 1963 was noticeable for two highlights in royal life, one pleasurable, the other less so. The pleasurable highlight was the marriage of the Queen's cousin, Princess Alexandra, to the Hon. Angus Ogilvy. The Queen threw a pre-wedding banquet and ball at Windsor, perhaps the most glittering night in the ancient castle's long history, for 1,600 guests, including sixty European royals. Philip, as offbeat as always, chartered a couple of coaches to take those same European royals on a magical mystery tour which included a pub lunch at Bray. A good time was had by all.

The same can hardly be said for the state visit of King Paul and Queen Frederika of Greece three months later. State visits are usually quiet, dignified affairs. Not this one. On the evening of the state banquet demonstrators tried to scale the spike-topped wall of the palace. One actually made it, only to end up under arrest along with ninety-four others. To prevent other demonstrators getting inside the Aldwych Theatre when the Queen took her Greek guests there to see *A Midsummer Night's Dream*, the Government bought up all the seats—1,012 of them—and handed out tickets to people selected by the Foreign Office. Even so, a Midsummer Night's Dream turned into something akin to a royal nightmare, with demonstrators greeting the Queen and her party with cries of " Sieg Heil " and " Nazis out." Scuffles with the police resulted in nine more arrests.

Anne was thirteen the year she went to Benenden. Charles was nearly fifteen and already taller than his mother. Andrew was three and a half . . . and the Queen was again pregnant.

Indeed, the early months of the following year proved exceptionally busy ones for the royal birds and bees. Princess Alexandra who has perhaps lost out on gifts over the years because Christmas Day is also her birthday, gave birth to a son, James, who may fare no better. He was born on 29th February—Leap Year's Day. Three other royal babies were ushered into the world hard on his heels. The Queen had her fourth child, Edward, on 10th March; the Duchess of Kent her second, Helen, on 28th April; and Princess Margaret her second, Sarah, on 1st May.

But if babies were being born, death was also claiming loyal and trusted friends. And none had been more loyal or trusted than Winston Churchill, the Prime Minister who had greeted the Queen with tears streaming down his cheeks when she flew into London on her Accession. His death, in January 1965, was perhaps the end of an era.

Normally the Queen attends the funerals only of royal relatives. Without some such restriction, she could find herself attending a funeral every week of the year. But Churchill's funeral was clearly in a category of its own. It was attended not only by the Queen, but by all save the very youngest members of the Royal Family as well as by five other monarchs, six additional heads of state and sixteen prime ministers. The Queen's all-white wreath of freesias, arum lilies, gladioli and lilies-of-the-valley had a card attached in her own writing: " From the Nation and the

Commonwealth. In grateful remembrance. Elizabeth R."

Churchill was dead and the Duke of Windsor, now over seventy, in declining health. Making a rare visit to Britain, he entered the London Clinic to undergo eye surgery. The Queen, anxious to heal the split in the family which had started with the Abdication, nearly thirty years before, was the first of the Royals to visit him. Waiting for her at the Duke's bedside, as the Queen had known she would be, was the woman for whom the ageing Duke had given up his throne. It was the first time the two of them had met since the Queen was a girl of ten.

The Queen's visit was not listed in the *Court Circular*. A palace spokesman, attempting to explain this away, called it " a personal and family matter." Yet it was surely more than that. The Queen would hardly have considered it necessary to have her Private Secretary along on something which was strictly personal and purely family . . . unless perhaps she expected her uncle to raise yet again the delicate question of elevating his wife to the rank of Royal Highness. And did he? Royal papers being sifted by some future biographer may one day reveal what happened.

Others of the Royal Family also visited the Duke while he was in the London Clinic, among them his sister, the Princess Royal, and his sister-in-law, Princess Marina, the widow of the dead brother to whom he was once so close. It was the last time he was to see his sister. She died unexpectedly only two weeks later. The Queen Mother, apparently still unforgiving after all those years, did not visit him.

In the double life which the Queen is sometimes forced to lead as monarch on the one hand and woman, wife and mother on the other, few things have been affected so much as her relationship with Philip's sisters. As his wife, she was their sister-in-law. As Queen, they (because all three were married to Germans) were her ex-enemies. For the first thirteen years of monarchy, and before that as the King's daughter, she had to walk the tricky tightrope which swung between. Though she was marrying their brother, she could not invite them to the wedding of 1947. Subsequently, she did have them to stay with her from time to time, but such visits must always be treated as " private " with as little said about them as possible. Publicity could start an uproar. And even privately she could not go to Germany to visit them in return. Philip could. The children could. But not the Queen.

Philip, free to say things which the Queen cannot, made an oblique reference to this odd state of affairs when addressing the Anglo-German Association in 1960. "Although forgiving one's enemies may be difficult for some people to visualize, it is more likely to achieve a better future than stoking the fires of hatred and suspicion."

That was said fifteen years after the end of World War II. For Britain, it was still too soon. It achieved nothing—except a sharp rap over the knuckles for Philip himself.

But by 1965 there was a policy of rapprochement between the former enemies and a state visit to Germany would help cement it. So off to Germany went the Queen and in her time off from official engagements she was finally free to visit her sisters-in-law in their homes at Salem and Langenburg.

If the Queen, visiting Germany on that occasion, was acting only as " a civil servant with a crown on her head," she has not always been content to be simply a monarchical rubber stamp, as she showed soon afterwards. While declining to appeal to the Rhodesian people over the heads of their leaders following that country's unilateral declaration of independence, she did send Ian Smith a personal letter reminding him of his duty to the Crown. And when Smith appointed his own " Governor " in place of hers, she riposted by making the legal Governor, Humphrey Gibbs, a Knight Grand Cross of the Royal Victorian Order, significantly one of the few honours in her personal gift.

Each morning, as she had done through all her years of monarchy, the Queen telephoned her mother at Clarence House for a brief mother-and-daughter chat. The Queen Mother was sixty-five that year of the Rhodesian upset, seemingly as fit, tireless and ageless as ever. There had been one or two causes for slight concern from time to time—a cracked bone caused by a fall at Windsor in 1961; an appendectomy in 1964—but nothing serious. But all at once, in December, 1966, the Queen had cause to worry about her mother.

A hospital check-up revealed a partial obstruction necessitating abdominal surgery, and it was a measure of this remarkable woman's continued popularity that during her three weeks in hospital letters and get-well cards streamed in from all parts of the world, sometimes in excess of a thousand a day. Thankfully, she made a quick recovery and shortly after Christmas was again well enough to leave London and join the rest of the family at Sandringham.

The Windsors were again in London in 1967, this time by the Queen's own invitation. The occasion was the unveiling of a memorial to Queen Mary, the Duke's mother and the Queen's grandmother. The Queen placed one of her cars at their disposal while they were in Britain and sent them back to their French home afterwards in an aircraft of the Queen's Flight. Even the Queen Mother relented sufficiently to accept a kiss from her brother-in-law and a handshake from his wife. But there was still no elevation to the style of Royal Highness for the Duchess and the interviewer who talked to the couple on television was noticeably careful to refer to her only as " Your Grace " while addressing the Duke as " Your Royal Highness."

In the fifteen years the Queen had now been on the throne the old guard of advisers she had inherited from her father had largely disappeared to be replaced by a set of younger, more with-it aides. From these emerged the idea that the Royal Family should take full advantage of today's television era. The outcome was the film *Royal Family*. If some critics were unkind enough to re-title it *Corgi and Beth* (after the American musical of somewhat similar title), it was nevertheless a resounding success with the public in general who relished the opportunity to peek behind the scenes at Royal Family picnics and tea-parties. American viewers in particular, when the film was shown over there, were surprised and delighted to realize that there was a real woman, human and down-to-earth with a lively sense of fun, behind the regal image.

That the Queen herself judged it to have been a success can be gauged from the fact that her Christmas telecast the following year was turned into what Prince Philip referred to, rather irreverently, as " The Queen Show." That year the Queen's traditional Christmas message became a television travelogue with snippets of film showing the royals aboard their yacht, at a garden party in Edinburgh, in Australia and among the Eskimos of the Canadian North.

One by one, the years of family life, along with the years of monarchy, were slipping by, each to some extent like the one before, but each different. Andrew was now old enough to go to boarding school and there was hardly any of the fanfare which had been heard when the school experiment was first attempted with Charles. The widowed Princess Marina, at whose wedding in 1934 the young Elizabeth had been a bridesmaid, died in her sixties. Philip's sister, Theodora, fifteen years his senior, also died in her sixties. His mother died at the age of eighty-four. Philip had flown out to Germany from Balmoral some three years before to bring her to London for medical treatment and, unknown to the general public, she had been living with her daughter-in-law at Buckingham Palace ever since, occupying the Buhl Suite in which her grandson, Prince Charles, was born.

The biggest slice of royal ceremonial since the Coronation saw Charles invested as Prince of Wales at Caernarvon.* Anne, by now, was through with boarding school. With no desire to follow Charles to university, she embarked instead on a career of royal chores, emerging as a combination of white-gloved princess, horse-riding tomboy and mini-skirted dolly bird which, initially, was like a fresh breeze blowing across the calm surface of the traditional royal round. She played tea parties with the tots in a children's home, slewed a police car round a greasy skid pan, sampled rum aboard a naval frigate, dropped in on a North Sea gas rig by helicopter and, visiting an army unit in Germany, drove a 52-ton tank and fired a burst from a sub-machine gun clapped to her hip. She danced in discothèques, bought a blouse in an Oxford Street chain store, went to way-out shows like *Hair* and joked about her underwear in a public speech. Her parents, incidentally, were not at all annoyed by the speech, as was said in some quarters at the time. Although she wrote it herself, she cleared it with them before delivery. She was twice stopped by the police for speeding in her sports car. If the long-running royal serial story was in danger of flagging, this was the stuff to pep it up.

Then all at once, perhaps because she was going through a difficult phase in her personal life, it all seemed to go wrong for a time. She was accused of being "rude" in Australia for saying that she would not want to live there, "sulky" in Canada after the embarrassment of having to clamber on to a too-high jetty in a too-short skirt. She was labelled "snobbish and spoilt" in the

* Chapter 8.

United States and "arrogant" in Kenya. At home, after an incident at the Burghley horse trials, photographers dubbed her "unco-operative".

But all was immediately forgiven her, at least for a time, when she won the European Three-Day Event Championship. Charles gained his R.A.F. "wings" around the same time and it was another sign of the passage of the years that Philip was reluctantly compelled to call a halt to his polo-playing. Not because he could no longer afford it, as one might have gathered from a remark he made on a U.S. television show, but because of recurring wrist trouble.

Like her mother, Anne has always been mad about horses. Had she been born other than royal, she might well have ended up as a professional show jumper or a bareback rider in a travelling circus. Riding, as she told her parents soon after leaving school, "is the one thing I do well and can be seen to do well." Certainly she did well enough to beat the cream of Britain, France, Italy, Ireland and Russia despite a spell in hospital for the removal of an ovarian cyst only weeks before. Hand and leg muscles, so important to anyone who rides competitively, had softened while in hospital. She toughened her hands with endless games of deck tennis, her legs by running up and down Scottish hillsides, thus displaying the "steely determination" which, according to her trainer, Alison Oliver, is among her principal assets.

This same "steely determination" could not quite bring her another victory in the same event when she went to Germany four years later as a member of Britain's official all-girl team, but it did much towards enabling her to haul herself up from equal ninth after the dressage to finish finally in second place to her team-mate, Lucinda Prior-Palmer.

It was Anne's love of horses which led to her romance with Mark Philips. He was a member of Britain's official team, which Anne was not, the year she won the European championship at Burghley. He had twice beaten her in previous equestrian events and during subsequent meetings at various horse trials and the concurrent social round, the friendly rivalry existing between them ripened into friendship and then love. In 1972, though she was not picked for Britain's Olympic team, Anne flew to Munich to watch Mark in action. That November she invited him to the party she and Charles gave to mark their parents' silver wedding anniversary. Among the other guests they invited were Princess Beatrix of the Netherlands, King Constantine and Queen Anne-Marie, and Prince Rainier and Princess Grace.

The Queen's silver wedding day was also marked by a state drive to Westminster Abbey for a thanksgiving service, a walk-about (the first in Britain) at the Barbican and a celebration lunch at the Guildhall. Perhaps because the occasion touched her so deeply, her speech on that occasion was one of the best she has made during her years of monarchy. Space permits only a short extract.

" A marriage begins by joining man and wife together. But this relationship, however deep, needs to develop and mature with the passing years. For that it must be held firm in the web of family relationships, between parents and children, grand-parents and grandchildren, cousins, aunts and uncles."

Few would deny that the Queen's own marriage has been held abundantly firm in this fashion. So she could add, with simplicity and conviction, " If I am asked what I think about family life after twenty-five years of marriage, I can answer : I am for it."

But the " web of family relationships " is an ever-changing one and the Royal Family web had already undergone further changes that year. In May, the Duke of Windsor had died at his home in Paris a few weeks before his seventy-eighth birthday. The Queen had last seen her uncle ten days earlier when, taking time out during another state visit to France, she had climbed the stairs in company with Philip and Charles (the Duke was too ill to come down) to visit him at his home. His body was brought back to Britain for burial. His widow came too, staying at Buckingham Palace for the first time and sitting between the Queen and Prince Philip for the funeral service in St. George's Chapel.

The Duke had been in failing health for some time and his death was perhaps not unexpected. More of a shock, three months later, was the death of the Queen's cousin, Prince William of Gloucester, at the youthful age of thirty. He was perhaps the most adventurous of the trio of wartime babies which also in-cluded his brother Richard and his cousin, Michael of Kent. His physical adventures included a camera safari to Ethiopia where he was charged by a wild buffalo. Education adventures included a year at America's Stanford University. With no wish to settle for a life of royal chores, he took a trainee job with a merchant bank. Later, switching to a diplomatic career and given a posting to Britain's embassy in Tokyo, he piloted his own plane on the long flight to Japan. There were also not a few romantic adventures.

After his father suffered a stroke in 1968 he gave up his diplomatic career in order to run the family estate at Barnwell Manor near Peterborough. His enthusiasm for flying was undiminished and in the 1971 King's Cup air race he finished in seventh place. In the July of 1972 he was best man when his brother Richard married Birgitte van Deurs, a Danish girl he had met while at Cambridge University. Six weeks after his brother's wedding William entered another air race. He had just taken off from Halfpenny Green, near Wolverhampton, in his Piper Cherokee when the machine banked sharply, struck a tree, plunged into a bank and exploded in flames.

The Queen was at Sandringham as usual for the New Year following her silver wedding anniversary. Again the wheel of family life had come full circle. More than quarter of a century before it had been Philip, as suitor for the hand of the then Princess Elizabeth, who had been invited to Sandringham. Now it was the Queen's turn to invite the young man her daughter wished to marry. In doing so, she had few, if any, of the qualms her father had experienced before her. The late King, as he told a friend, always found it difficult to realize that his daughter had fallen in love with the first eligible young man she had met. But where Anne was concerned, there had been not a few eligible young men over the years, and Mark, the Queen felt, was " right " for her.

In public life it may be necessary for Philip to take second place to his wife, as Queen. But in their private life the Queen has always accorded him what she considers to be his rightful place as husband, father and head of the family. So it was to Philip and not the Queen, at Windsor some months later, that Mark Phillips addressed his request for Anne's hand in marriage. He was, to use his own word, " petrified ".

They were married at Westminster Abbey in November 1973. Palace officials, with their own curious outlook on things, described the wedding as " private ". With 4,000 police on duty, five military bands and 1,600 guests, including twenty-five foreign royals, it was in fact a combination of state ceremony and television spectacular with a touch of musical comedy thrown in for good measure. Among those present was the Queen Mother, of course. For her it was part of another busy month during which she planted a cross in the British Legion Field of Remembrance, attended a reception at the University of London in her role of Chancellor, visited Oxford, where she unveiled a bust of Field Marshal Alexander of Tunis, and Leeds, where, characteristically, she rummaged around in her handbag to find a throat lozenge for a seaman who had lost his voice.

Like most mums, the Queen seemed tense until the wedding ceremony was all but over, when she smiled for the first time and gave her new son-in-law what looked suspiciously like a royal wink. In small things as in large history continued to repeat itself. " Don't forget to salute," the Queen had reminded Philip years before as they drove past the Cenotaph on their way to board their honeymoon train. Now it was daughter Anne's turn. " Be ready to acknowledge the crowds," she whispered to Mark as they emerged from Westminster Abbey.

In a sense, the newlyweds had the benefit of two honeymoons. The first was aboard the royal yacht where, in the absence of a double bed, two single ones were lashed together for them. The second, soon after, came when they flew out to New Zealand to join the bride's parents and brother Charles for what the Queen herself happily referred to as " a family gathering."

Friends of the bridegroom who feared that he might prove " too shy " for the royal round were quickly disillusioned. Indeed, in New Zealand and elsewhere, he revealed a touch of Prince Philip. Given a garland of carrots with which to decorate the winning pony at a horse show, he promptly proceeded to feed the carrots to the animal. Elsewhere, presented with a basket of tropical fruit, he spotted one shaped rather like a microphone. Taking it out of the basket, he held it towards the nearest commentator. " Care to say a few words?" he invited him.

Hardly was the Queen back from this tour of New Zealand, Australia and the Pacific than she was off again, this time on a state visit to Indonesia. And it was while she was in Jakarta that a telephone call from Buckingham Palace informed her of the horrifying attempt to kidnap Princess Anne.

Anne and Mark were returning from a charity film show and

were within sight of Buckingham Palace when another driver cut in front of them and forced their car to a halt. A man got out and ran back, gun in hand. In the next few nightmare minutes the royal chauffeur, Alex Callender, Anne's bodyguard, Inspector James Beaton, a policeman, Michael Hills, and a passing journalist, Brian McConnell, were all gunned down. The gunman wrenched open the rear door of the car, seized Anne by the wrist and tried to drag her out. Despite Mark's efforts to prevent him, he might have succeeded but for the timely intervention of Ron Russell, a burly Cockney, who waded in with his fists, knocking him down and delaying him sufficiently for police reinforcements to arrive.

" It was incredible," Anne told her mother, describing the incident on the Queen's return. " The sort of thing one can't believe is really happening."

Later that year came the death of the last of the Queen's uncles, the Duke of Gloucester. He was seventy-four and had been in failing health for several years. His elder son have predeceased him, the younger, Richard, a partner in a London firm of architects, became the new Duke of Gloucester at the age of twenty-nine. Four months later Richard's Danish-born wife gave birth to their first child, Alexander.

At the time of Anne's marriage the Queen was heard to express a not unnatural hope that she might become a grandmother before " I am too old to enjoy it." A small incident in the summer of 1975 set people wondering if her wish was to be granted.

It happened when Anne and Mark visited the church fête in his home village of Great Somerford. Among the items on display was an embroidered tapestry depicting their wedding. " We don't know what we are going to do for next year," remarked one of the good ladies who had worked on the tapestry.

It was Mark's reply—" You will have to do something for the christening "—which set the village and, subsequently, the nation twittering.

But it would seem that he was again merely modelling himself on father-in-law Prince Philip, who has also made some pretty straight-faced jokes in his time, and a palace spokesman quickly put things in perspective by pointing out that Anne was due to compete in a three-day event in the United States . . . and she would hardly do that " if she were pregnant, would she?" Time has since justified the comment.

In many ways, 1975 was another year of controversy for the Queen. Willie Hamilton, not content with his usual blunt comments when the new Civil List was debated in Parliament,* also wrote a book entitled *My Queen and I* which brought ardent royalists to the verge of apoplexy. A film company used some old newsreel footage of the Queen skilfully edited to make it seem that she was acting opposite Rod Steiger playing the role of a latter-day Guy Fawkes about to blow up Parliament. The Queen, though she had orginally given permission for the footage to be used, objected once she heard how it had been used. All a " misunderstanding," said the palace, though no fault of the film company. Misunderstanding was corrected by an agreed statement being shown with the credits to make it clear that the shots of the Queen were " extracts from a news film . . . not intended for use in a fictional context."

With this film still going the rounds, another company also decided to cash in on the royal act with a French-made comedy in which an ageing Mickey Rooney played the part of a man who falls in love with the Queen and kidnaps her. Newsreel shots of the real Queen being clearly unsuitable in this context, even if obtainable after the previous furore, the film company fell back on the services of a woman with the improbable name of Huguette Funfrock who had previously won a French newspaper competition to find the Queen's double.

" There is nothing we can do about it," sighed Buckingham Palace, resignedly.

On top of all this, and a good deal more serious, was the ugly business of Uganda's President Amin and his threat to execute British lecturer Denis Hills for calling him " a village tyrant " unless Foreign Secretary James Callaghan flew out to Uganda to see him, all Uganda exiles were deported from Britain, etcetera, etcetera, etcetera.

Presumably acting on the advice of her prime minister, Harold Wilson, the Queen again attempted to intervene as she had done with Ian Smith over Rhodesia. In her capacity as Head of the Commonwealth, she wrote a personal letter to the Ugandan

* Chapter 11.

leader and sent it by the hand of Lieutenant-General Sir Chandos Blair, who was Amin's commanding officer when he was a sergeant in the King's African Rifles. Amin's reaction was perhaps predictable in its unpredictability. After welcoming the Queen's messenger with declarations of presidential affection, he was soon accusing him of being " drunk, hot-tempered, undiplomatic and disrespectful." The General returned to London with a letter for the Queen which was read over the telephone to her at Balmoral, where she was staying. Hot on its heels came yet another lengthy epistle from Amin, the crux of which was that he was postponing the execution of Hills because "of the love, confidence and respect which I and the entire people of Uganda have for you as leader of Great Britain and the Commonwealth."

However, while he seemed to have dropped his other demands, he was still insisting on the Foreign Secretary going to Uganda. Callaghan did so by way of Zaire, employing a diplomatic face-saving device to sustain the fact that he was not acting under duress . . . and the pawn in this game of twisting the British lion's tail was finally released.

But if there were several such upsets for the Queen that year of 1975, there was also one cause at least for celebration. On 4th August the woman Willie Hamilton once referred to as Princess Margaret's " old mum " and who most of us think of as the Queen Mum celebrated her seventy-fifth birthday. " Happy birthday, dear Mother," sang the small crowd which gathered outside Clarence House to mark the occasion. " Happy birthday to you."

That the Queen Mother is ostentatious and perhaps extravagant can hardly be denied. That she more than any other established the monarchy on an even keel again after the upset of the abdication is equally undeniable. Her husband, on his own admission, could not have managed it on his own. You balance one against the other and decide on which side the scales hang lower.

Over the years since her husband's death the Queen Mother has been as energetic and hard-working on her daughter's behalf as she was in support of him. There was a period following his death when it seemed that she might retire from public life and nurse her grief, as Queen Victoria did, in solitude and privacy. It was while this emotion was dominant that she bought the Castle of Mey in the north of Caithness, about as far removed from public life as you can hope to get. But solitude, she quickly found, was not for her. While she had originally hesitated to marry into the Royal Family because, as she said, it would mean that she no longer had a life of her own, now she found that she could no longer live without people. So bit by bit, while she kept her husband's desk at Royal Lodge set out just as it was in his lifetime, she took up the threads of public living again.

At the ripe old age of seventy-three she was still carrying out public engagements at the rate of three a week. By seventy-five the pace had slackened somewhat to around a hundred engagements a year, which was still pretty good going for a woman of her age. Among other things, during the twelve months preceding her seventy-fifth birthday, she flew out to Germany to present shamrocks to the Irish Guards on St Patrick's Day, visited Iran and Cyprus, the Channel Isles and the Isle of Wight. Standing in for her daughter while the Queen was in Mexico, she acted as Counsellor of State, signing state papers and holding two investitures. She reluctantly admitted to getting a little tired sometimes, but there were no signs of tiredness as she whirled round the dance floor in the Gay Gordons at the London University ball.

It would be tedious to list all her public functions that year, but it is perhaps appropriate to mention those in her beloved Scotland. She opened a new hospital in Dundee (where she also installed the new rector of the university) and the Aboyne Academy in Aberdeenshire. She visited Edinburgh and Fife as part of the European Architectural Heritage Year. She was again in Edinburgh to attend the Thistle Service at St Giles' cathedral, a reception at the Edinburgh Angus Club, to open the Stockbridge Day Centre and to hear the Scottish Division beat the retreat in Holyrood Park. She attended the graduation ceremony at Dundee University, a flower show in Aberdeen, a thanksgiving service in Kirkwall and played her part during the visit of King Carl Gustaf of Sweden to the Palace of Holyroodhouse.

On her seventy-fifth birthday gifts, bouquets and cards inundated Clarence House, all—even those from strangers—to be meticulously acknowledged. What the family gave her remained a close-kept secret, with one small exception. From grandson Andrew there was a dish and a vase which he had turned on the potter's wheel at Gordonstoun.

And three days after the Queen Mother's birthday, in the House of Commons, came the first official mention of the occasion for which this book has been written—the Queen's Silver Jubilee. The Government, said Roy Jenkins, the Home Secretary, was considering how the occasion could best be marked bearing in mind the Queen's wish that "undue expenditure should be avoided."

Undue expenditure may be easy enough to avoid. Unpleasant publicity is another matter and there was to be a further spate of it as the Queen entered upon the twenty-fifth year of her monarchy. At the centre of the vortex again, as she had been in Coronation year, was Princess Margaret. Then it had been because of her romance with Peter Townsend. Now it was because of her separation from Lord Snowdon. For several years their marriage had been under strain, subject to continuing gossip as to who was doing what and where and when. More than once there had been speculation about possible divorce. So news that they were separating was hardly a surprise.

It was all very civilized. Margaret was to keep both the matrimonial home at Kensington Palace and the children, but Tony would have unlimited access. So civilized, in fact, that separated husband and wife were both guests at the party the Queen gave at Windsor a few weeks later to celebrate her fiftieth birthday, though the new Prime Minister, James Callaghan, was not. He was too busy to get along, he said.

The Queen's birthday party started with dinner for sixty on the evening of 20th April. A further five hundred guests were invited for the ball which followed and at 2.40 a.m. precisely on 21st April—the exact moment of her birth—a radiantly happy Elizabeth took the floor with husband Philip to the music of Joe Loss. Her sister's marriage might have run on the rocks, but the Queen's, clearly, was sailing along as smoothly as ever after more than twenty-eight years.

The new Queen in Edinburgh

The Queen's guests at a dinner party. The Commonwealth Ministers attending the Economies Conference in London in 1952 were (from left to right): Mr D. S. Senanayake (Ceylon), Sir Godfrey Huggins (Rhodesia), Mr Holland (New Zealand), Mr Churchill (Great Britain), Mr Menzies (Australia), Mr St Laurent (Canada), Mr Havenga (S. Africa), Mr Khawaja Nazimuddin (Pakistan) and Sir Chintaman Deshmukh (India)

The Queen's first
Christmas broadcast, 1952

Rewarded for her long
wait, this old lady talks to
the Queen. New Zealand,
1954

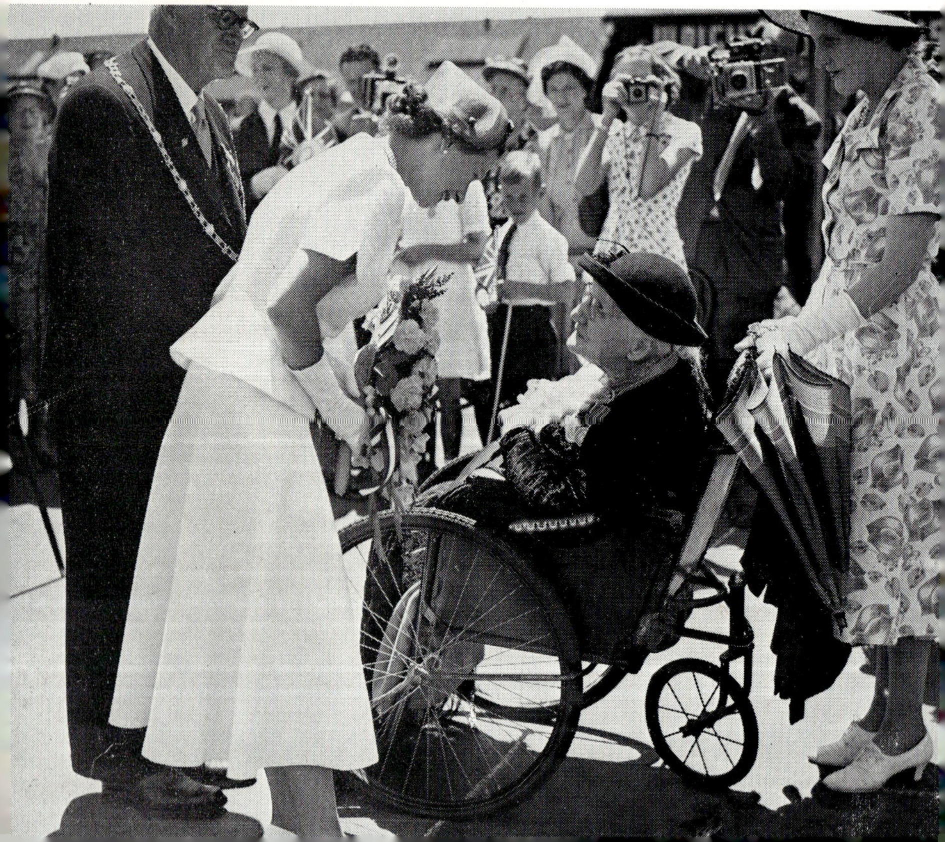

6

The Queen's Travels

Because no one—not even royal aides—has kept count, no one knows for certain how much mileage the Queen has covered during her years of monarchical globetrotting. After only seven years of her reign she was already the most-travelled monarch in Britain's history. Of the first ten years, she spent over a year out of the country. That, of course, includes the six months taken up by the 44,000-mile round-the-world trip she undertook soon after her Coronation.

There has been no other trip of such magnitude since; nor is there likely to be in the future, though there are some impressive figures over the years: 18,000 miles across Canada and back when she was pregnant with Andrew in 1959, a 15,000-mile figure-of-eight tour of India, Pakistan and Nepal in 1961, a round trip of 25,000 miles to visit Malaysia, Singapore, Brunei and the Seychelles in 1972. While no one can provide us with an exact figure, our own estimate of the Queen's total mileage to date puts it at 400,000, give or take a thousand or two, or more than sixteen times the circumference of the world.*

Over the years she has been injected against polio, smallpox, typhoid, yellow fever and goodness only knows what else. She has travelled by train and plane, by royal yacht and royal barge, by gondola (in Venice, where else?) and rubber dinghy. She travelled in an old-fashioned open charabanc in Portugal, drove through Quebec in a bullet-proof limousine and was hauled around in Brunei in a golden chariot drawn by forty-eight hefty warriors.

She has been greeted by people wearing everything from saris to swimsuits; addressed as everything from Your Majesty to

* Appendix III.

Missus Kwin (her Pidgin English title in New Guinea). In Ghana they even called her Lizzie. She has experienced almost every extreme of climatic conditions, from the deep-freeze of the Canadian Arctic to the steam-heat of Sri Lanka, to say nothing of enduring the plague of flies which infest the baked Kalgoorlie goldfields in Australia.

At Kalgoorlie, while the mining area had been drenched with insecticide ahead of the Queen's visit, they had somehow over-looked the air strip. In no time at all, the light-coloured clothes worn by the reception committee and the Queen's own entourage had turned almost black under the swarm of flies which settled on them. But the Queen, wearing darker clothes, was relatively un-troubled.

" I must have been psychic," she joked.

She has watched sheep shearing in Australia and fertility rites in New Britain. She was watching a particularly spectacular display on Pentecost Island, where young men dived from a seventy-foot tower with jungle vines tied to their ankles to check their fall, when one of the vines snapped and the unfortunate diver smashed into the ground only feet from where she was standing, killing himself.

She has heard Maori war chants in New Zealand and American football chants in the United States. She has walked on coconut matting as well as red carpets, had her health drunk in everything from champagne to coconut milk, been serenaded by hymns and calypsos, entertained by war drums, nose flutes and cow-horn trumpets. She has feasted on everything from the curry and curd dishes of India to raw fish in Tonga. She has tasted hotdogs in Chicago and *coco-de-mer*, the legendary forbidden fruit of the Garden of Eden, in the Seychelles. She has eaten with her fingers in Fiji and tried out chopsticks in Singapore. She found that she could not manage them and switched to a spoon instead.

As Monarch, she has opened Parliament in places as far apart as Canada and Australia, Malta and New Zealand. In 1974 she opened no fewer than three separate Parliaments—in London, Wellington and Canberra—in little more than five weeks. She has flown over Everest; sailed both the Caribbean and the South Seas. In Africa she has visited Nigeria, Ghana, Liberia, Sierra Leone, Gambia, Kenya, Libya and the Sudan. She has been to

Turkey and Iran, India, Pakistan and Nepal, Malaysia, Indonesia and Japan. She has been to Canada and the United States, Mexico, Brazil and Chile. And all this without once producing a passport. As British passports are issued in her name, she does not need one, though Philip does.

But though she does not require a passport, the Queen is not a free agent when it comes to overseas travel; nor are her world-wide journeys mere holiday jaunts. Her trips reflect the foreign policy of the British Government and she can go only to those foreign countries of which the Government approves (though the Government has no say when it comes to visiting those other countries of the Commonwealth of which she is also Queen). For this reason, she has never—up to the time this book was being written—been to Spain, though thousands of her subjects spend their vacations there each year. Nor since she became Queen has she been back to South Africa, though her twenty-first birthday was celebrated there. Though she has been several times to the United States, she has yet to go to Russia. There have been behind-the-scenes approaches from Moscow since Philip went there (and to Kiev) in 1973 and if the *détente* between East and West continues the Queen may yet follow in her husband's footsteps. In 1972 she did go to communist Yugoslavia where she was greeted by large crowds and enthusiastic applause, neither of which was perhaps completely spontaneous. Yet certainly the polite behaviour of the clean-cut and possibly hand-picked students who welcomed her to Belgrade university was in vivid contrast to the bad manners shown by the long-haired yobs at Scotland's Stirling university only a week before.

Over her years of monarchy the Queen has paid state visits to most of the countries of Europe as well as to Mexico, Japan and other places afield. A state visit, as the name implies, is a courtesy call which one head of state pays on another. It lasts, usually, no more than three days. If the Queen stays longer, as she did in Germany (to visit her sisters-in-law) and in France (to see some horses), it is in a private capacity.

The programme for a state visit will usually include an official welcome, a ceremonial drive through the capital of the country concerned, some sightseeing on a cultural and historic level, a visit to the ballet, opera or similar, a state banquet given by the Queen's host and a reciprocal function on her side, either at the local British embassy or aboard the royal yacht.

Most of these ingredients were to be found in the programme when, in 1975, the Queen became the first reigning British monarch to visit Japan. There was an opening state drive through Tokyo streets miraculously cleared of traffic in a bullet-proof car provided by the security-conscious Japanese. Later, at the Queen's request, an open-top vehicle was substituted so that people could see her better. There was a banquet with Emperor Hirohito at the Imperial State Palace, a meeting with members of the Diet (Japan's Parliament), lunch with businessmen and union representatives, visits to the Commonwealth war cemetery at Hodogaya and the Shinto shrine at Ise, and a cup of the traditional green tea at Kyoto. The tea caused even the Queen's celebrated sang-froid to desert her for once. She was seen to grimace slightly as she tasted it and made only a one-word reference to what she thought of it: " Surprising." She enjoyed a trip in one of Japan's 125 m.p.h. super-speed trains and watched girl pearl divers at work at Toba. As all followers of James Bond know, Japanese pearl girls normally dive topless. Out of respect for the Queen, they covered themselves with thin cotton overalls on the occasion of her visit. Which was fine, until the overalls got wet—and semi-transparent. The Queen hastily averted her gaze while Philip grinned.

Tours of those countries of which she is Queen or, at very least, accepted as Head of the Commonwealth, last longer than a state visit and cast a wider net. The object in this case is to let the Queen see something of the country concerned and let the inhabitants see her in return. Instead of simply staying in the capital, she embarks on what Americans know as a " whistle-stop " tour. She is welcomed at each fresh stopping-place by the local mayor or his equivalent and a supporting cast of eager-beaver local dignitaries. She will listen to a speech of welcome, accept a bouquet of flowers or an illuminated address, make a short speech of thanks, perhaps inspect a guard of honour or plant a commemoration tree (which means that she tosses in the first few handfuls of soil and then passes the spade to someone else to finish the job).

She may visit a local school, hospital or factory; perhaps all three in the larger centres. In the cities there will also be a civic luncheon or banquet, perhaps a garden party, barbecue or ball.

In addition, there will usually be some form of open-air gathering specially for children.

In recent years there has been an attempt to reduce the inevitable formality of her public appearances by the inclusion of what are called "walkabouts", casual and unrehearsed strolls through the street with brief pauses to exchange hellos with whoever happens to be nearest and handiest. The first such "walkabout", in Australia in 1970, was hailed as something new and revolutionary. Commented the *Sydney Morning Telegraph*: "No more will they (the Royals) appear remote figures, removed from the realities which face ordinary men and women. They have been seen as warm and human, full of fun and laughter . . ."

In fact, the whole business was hardly as new and revolutionary as all that. Nearly forty years ago, visiting the World Fair in the pre-war spring of 1939, the Queen's mother ducked under the linked arms of New York's "Finest" to walk and talk with people who had turned out to see her.

For the Queen, however, that 1970 Australian walkabout did represent something new. There have been others since, at home and abroad, their very informality adding to her workload—it is much more of a strain to walk through a jostling crowd, pausing here and there to chat, than it is to drive past in a car or carriage—and increasing the tension of a basically shy woman. Yet the Queen is less concerned for herself than for those who throng to see her. She fears some will be hurt. And, indeed, after that first 1970 walkabout, when an estimated quarter of a million people jostled to see her, some were later treated for either exhaustion or broken bones. The Queen herself spotted one small boy crying because he had become separated from his parents in the crush. She asked one of her bodyguards to help and the resulting loudspeaker appeal saw kiddy and parents quickly reunited.

Even without walkabouts, the Queen's days on tour are long and full. In Hamilton, Bermuda, in the course of a single day, she inspected a guard of honour, visited the site of the first British Parliament outside Westminster, called in at a U.S. naval base and a U.S. air base, toured the main island by car, drove in an open carriage to the House of Assembly, addressed Parliament, went for a boat trip, planted a tree and attended both a garden party and a banquet.

After all this, the lights in Government House, where she spent the night, came on at quarter past four the following morning. By half-past five she was on her way to the airfield and at quarter to ten she was landing in Jamaica for more long full days . . . like the one in Kingston which started with a military parade at quarter past eight in the morning (because it would be too hot later) and ended with a reception which did not start until nine in the evening. The Queen crammed so many other engagements in between that, at one stage, she found herself with less than thirty minutes in which to wash, change, re-do her hair and freshen her make-up before attending an official lunch.

The following morning she was called in time to be at a polo game by half-past seven. But bad weather had set in during the night.

" I'm so tired I think I'll go back to bed," the Queen sighed with relief when she heard that the game was cancelled.

The average royal tour is certainly no relaxed sightseeing trip. It is a long hard, sometimes monotonous, grind with the same motions of hand-shaking and speech-making to be gone through each day. Sometimes several times a day. " We don't come here for our health," Philip reminded Canadians in 1969. " We can think of other ways of enjoying ourselves." In a week on tour the Queen will usually have less time off than the average office, shop or factory worker back home. On one tour of Australia, for instance, she had a total of eight and a half days off—six days and five half-days—in the course of two months. And between stops she sees less of the scenery than the maids and footmen travelling with her. She is too busy dealing with the contents of the diplomatic pouches which take the place of the traditional boxes.

Experience has taught her not a few tricks of the royal travel trade. She has developed a special wave to ease the strain on her arm muscles. Whenever possible, she props her elbow on an arm-rest to further ease the strain. Between stops, out of public view, she will nudge her shoes off and sit with her feet up. Philip, travelling by train on a whistle-stop tour, will sometimes stretch out full-length and take a cat-nap.

Barbra Streisand, presented to the Queen at a film premiere, asked her why she always wears gloves. Taken aback by the question, the Queen stammered out that she did not know, a reply which was perhaps more of a measurement of her inability to make small talk than a statement of fact. In fact, she wears gloves to protect her hands and prevent them being rubbed raw by excessive handshaking. She also employs the special, rather limp handshake, with the vulnerable little finger kept well out of harm's way, which her father devised after his hand was injured by too much handshaking in Swansea on one occasion.

The late King, on that occasion, shook hands with three hundred people. His daughter is either more skilful or a good deal tougher. She once shook hands with two thousand people at a reception in Washington and, we have been told, with twice that number in Rome. Only once has she been seen to wince. This was in Australia when her whole hand vanished into the huge, vice-like grip of a professional sheep-shearer.

Despite these tricks of the trade, the Queen usually returns from a royal tour noticeably slimmer than when she left home. Sometimes she looks strained too. And few trips have left her more strained than the forty-five-day tour of Canada undertaken when she was expecting Andrew.

The Canadian prime minister was unaware of her condition until she actually got there. And she insisted that he should tell no one else. Nor would she agree to any curtailing of her itinerary, and more and more, as the tour progressed, the strain told on her. It was hardly to be wondered at. In Toronto, instead of sitting with her feet up like most expectant mums, she was on the go for fourteen hours on a day when the thermometer hit 95 degrees in the shade. In Port Arthur she was caught in a rain squall and soaked through. In Vancouver, over a period of ten hours, she had only three short breaks totalling forty minutes in all. By the time she reached Whitehorse she was so exhausted that some of her entourage feared she would faint in public. Her physician insisted that she should spend a day in bed while Philip went on alone to Dawson City. But she still went to Edmonton and, unwell though she was, she then undertook a four-day whistle-stop tour of the Prairie Provinces. By the time that was done she was so worn out that, instead of returning home by sea as planned, it was considered advisable for her to fly back for an immediate medical check.

Of course, the Queen travels always in the grandest of grand manners. If she goes by train, she has a coach to herself. And one

that looks as little like an ordinary railway coach as the royal
yacht looks like a tramp steamer. It is divided into sitting-room,
bedroom and bathroom with further small rooms for her dresser
and footman. The sitting-room section has a desk at which the
Queen can work as she travels, two sofas, two matching armchairs and an occasional table usually topped with a vase of
flowers. If Philip accompanies her, he has a similar coach,
similarly divided, for his use.

For air travel in Britain there is the Queen's Flight, consisting
of three Hawker Siddeley 748s, each with accommodation for
fifteen to twenty people, and two Westland helicopters which
Philip uses rather more frequently than the Queen does. For
overseas trips the Queen will charter a jet-liner from British Air-
ways. This is usually adapted to provide her with a miniature
royal apartment, a diminutive dining-room seating perhaps eight
people, a small, comfortable sitting-room with divans which con-
vert into beds at night, and two tiny dressing-rooms with built-in
wardrobes.

Nothing is more calculated to throw Britain's left-wingers into
a tizzy than a mention of the royal yacht. Built at a cost of £2
million to replace the old unseaworthy *Victoria & Albert*, and
costing an estimated one and a half million more to operate
annually, *Britannia* bears as little resemblance to an ordinary
yacht as Buckingham Palace does to a suburban villa. Measuring
413 feet from stem to stern, with a mainmast so tall it had to be
hinged before the vessel could pass under the bridges of the St
Lawrence Seaway, the royal yacht is nothing less than a sea-going
palace.

A wide mahogany staircase leads down to an elegant drawing-
room into which scarcely a nautical note intrudes. Tall mahogany
doors link the drawing-room with the ante-room and these can
be folded back to form a single reception hall into which up to
two hundred guests can be entertained at a time. The dining-
room with its ebony-edged table is similarly magnificent. The
table was originally designed to seat thirty-two people, but Philip,
after taking a train-load of royal servants to Portsmouth for a
try-out, thought this too small. At his suggestion removable
wings were added enabling the dining-room to seat sixty guests
should the occasion arise. Wall panels can be slid aside to reveal
a screen if the room is required to serve as a private cinema.

The Queen and Prince Philip each have a private sitting-room off the ante-room. The Queen's room is essentially feminine, with white panelling, moss-green carpet, chintz curtains and silk-shaded wall lights. Philip's room, with its teak panels, grey carpet, functional lighting and concealed drinks cabinet, is robustly masculine. A model of the frigate *Magpie* which he commanded in his Navy days stands in an illuminated case above the electric fire. Each room has a built-in leather-topped desk.

An elevator connects the sitting-rooms with the royal bedrooms. On the same deck as the bedrooms is a wardrobe room for the Queen's clothes, cabins for her dresser and Philip's valet, and, overlooking the stern, a glass-enclosed sun lounge where the Queen likes to breakfast.

The windows of the bedrooms are set high enough to prevent members of the crew glancing in as they pussyfoot past in their rubbed-soled shoes. They are fitted with beds, not bunks. The Queen's bedroom has its dressing-table hooked to the wall and is rubber-topped to prevent brushes and combs skidding about in rough weather.

Even so, there was one occasion, during a stormy crossing of the North Sea, when the dressing-table broke loose from its moorings in the middle of the night, slid across the cabin and thumped into the Queen's bed.

" I thought we were under attack," the Queen joked, looking on in her dressing gown while members of the crew made the dressing-table fast again.

That was a long time ago, before the yacht was fitted with stabilizers. Even with stabilizers, the yacht dipped and lurched so much during a rough crossing from the north to the south island of New Zealand in 1970—three sailors were swept overboard from an accompanying frigate—that the Queen had to swallow some anti-seasick pills and take to her bed.

" I did not enjoy the experience," she said afterwards, with feeling.

Even a three-day state visit can involve several months of preparation and planning. A royal tour of any magnitude can be a year or more on the drawing board. The proposed itinerary is worked out by the country the Queen is visiting, with the details submitted for her approval at each fresh stage along the way. Consistently conscientious, she likes to check everything herself and will sometimes come up with an improving suggestion. Ahead of one visit to the United States, for instance, she noticed that it would be after dark when her aircraft touched down in Washington.

" Won't people be disappointed if they can't see me?" she queried. " Can't we land in daylight?" Plans for the trip were revised accordingly.

Equally, she likes to familiarize herself thoroughly with the places she will be seeing and people she will be meeting. Her aides help with this by preparing thumbnail sketches. Maps and books are also useful, and to Sandringham each New Year, for bedtime reading, she takes a pile of books dealing with those countries she will be visiting that year.

There is also the matter of a new wardrobe. For a royal tour of any length the Queen will need perhaps fifty or sixty different outfits if she is not to wear the same one too many times and is to have something suitable for each separate type of public engagement. For her comparatively brief state visit to Japan in 1975, for instance, she took with her thirty dresses designed by Norman Hartnell, Hardy Amies and Ian Thomas (who once worked for Hartnell and now has his own couture establishment), forty pairs of shoes, fifteen hats and four tiaras. And presumably fearing that even that lot might be insufficient, she had another evening dress, a day dress and a matching coat run up for her on the cheap in Hong Kong on the way out.

If a state banquet is on the itinerary, as in the case of Japan, then a state gown is, of course, a must. With its elaborate hand-worked embroidery usually embodying the national flower or emblem of the country she is visiting—cherry blossom for Japan, maple leaves for Canada, mimosa for Australia, poppies, corn-flowers and marguerites for France—a state gown can take several months to make and necessitate several fittings. Even more ordinary clothes must be designed to suit the climate of the country she is visiting and the time of year she will be there. They must also ensure that she is clearly visible from a distance, has freedom of movement and can climb in and out of cars with decorum.

In preparing a royal tour wardrobe, preliminary sketches are first drawn for the Queen's consideration. Each sketch is a miniature full-length portrait so that she can gauge how she will look in a particular outfit, with a swatch of the material attached. As the work progresses, fittings take up hours of her time. Whole afternoons may be spent in her dressing-room with the designer and his assistants bobbing and ducking around her. The fittings over, someone goes over the carpet with a magnet to retrieve any stray pins.

There are hats and shoes to be tried on, too. Usually the Queen has a matching pair of shoes made for each outfit, though with so much walking and standing, when the tour is actually in progress she naturally tends to cling to those few pairs she finds most comfortable. Sometimes, indeed, she will wear the same pair again and again, and so noticeable was this on one tour of Australia that a fashion writer queried: Has the Queen only one pair of shoes?

During the early years of her monarchy the Queen clung for perhaps too long to the old royal idea that wishy-washy pastel shades were best as they enabled her to be seen from a distance. She also stuck to the traditional royal styles favoured by her mother before her. Only rarely could she be persuaded otherwise and even then she would sometimes shy away at the last moment from anything she considered too exotic.

Her first state visit to France was a case in point. Among the clothes Hartnell made for that trip was a pencil-slim evening gown of silver lace over silver tissue, as unlike the traditional royal crinoline as a butterfly is unlike a moth. But in Paris, at the last moment, dressing for a night trip along the Seine, the Queen decided that it was too dramatic. She would wear a crinoline instead, she said.

It was left to her dresser, the faithful " Bobo " Macdonald, to persuade her otherwise. " You will have difficulty getting up the gangplank in a crinoline," she said. " It's rather narrow."

The Queen had already had problems with a crinoline when squeezing in and out of the rather small car the French had provided for her and Bobo's words did the trick. She wore the new dress and French newspapers the next day described her as " ravishing ", which is not a word often applied to the Queen.

She was so delighted that visiting France again fifteen years later, on the trip which heralded Britain's entry into the Common Market, she asked Hartnell to make her a very similar dress, again pencil-slim, but this time in silver tissue with silver and lace embroidery.

It was not until 1971, ahead of her visit to Turkey, that she finally gave way to Hartnell's reiterated plea for consistently brighter royal clothes. Since then she has become steadily more fashion conscious and the old moans that she tends to look "dowdy" no longer apply. Says John Fairchild, publisher of America's *Women's Wear Daily* : "Whenever I have seen her, she looks just like a Queen should look."

To understand the work involved ahead of a royal trip, let us look in brief detail at the planning for just one tour. To plan one of the Queen's cross-country treks of Canada, the Canadian Government called in a former chief of staff, Lieutenant-General Howard Graham. Working under him were four principal assistants, eight secretaries and clerks and seventy-four other people grouped into seven committees.

Advance planning included laying-on jet aircraft to get the contents of the Queen's boxes to her wherever she might be and other aircraft to leapfrog three royal cars across Canada ahead of her so that they were available at each fresh stopping place. Arrangements had to be made for even such things as dry-cleaning the Queen's clothes and laundering the royal smalls.

Maps, plans, correspondence and proposed schedules shuttled back and forth between Lieutenant-General Graham in Ottawa, the Canadian High Commissioner's office in London, the Commonwealth Office and Buckingham Palace. The proposed route was marked out on a map six feet square and this was sent to the Queen. Opening it up, she found it too big for her desk. She spread it out on the sitting-room carpet instead and she and Philip crawled round it on their hands and knees.

Canada's Under-Secretary for External Affairs twice flew the Atlantic to discuss things with the Queen and her aides. Then a party of royal aides flew out to Canada for a dummy run. Wherever the Queen goes, a similar party, usually consisting of the Master of the Household, one of her Assistant Private Secretaries and one of the royal bodyguards, goes over the ground ahead of her. The Private Secretary times the itinerary at each stopping place. The bodyguard checks on security arrangements. The Master of the Household copes with the many questions posed by those who will be hosting the Queen. Does she like caviar? No.

Oysters? No. What sort of pillows does she like? She'll be bringing her own. Is it correct that she prefers orange juice to anything else to drink? No, orange squash.

The Queen, he tells them, prefers to sleep with her bed-head against a wall; she likes a full-length mirror in which she can inspect herself from top to toe before going out; and she will need a desk at which she can work between public functions. Philip, he informs them, prefers a shower to a bath and likes a big bed in which to stretch out at night. In Washington he got it—the massive eight-footer once used by Abraham Lincoln.

Despite such careful advance planning, things sometimes go wrong. During her 1972 visit to Yugoslavia, for instance, the Queen landed at Dubrovnick to find that the reception committee, guard of honour and embassy officials had switched to Titograd, a hundred miles away, under the impression that her aircraft was being diverted there because of bad weather.

Those acting as hosts to the Queen often interpret the request for a desk as referring to something small, dainty and elegant. What the Queen actually needs is something affording the largest possible working space. When her hosts come up with something inadequate, it is left to her staff to remedy the mistake and they did so on one occasion by commandeering a large dining table and manhandling it into her sitting-room.

The Queen's personal staff—her dresser, page and footman—are resourceful in the extreme. They arrived at one small hotel at which the Queen was spending the night to find that the customary full-length mirror had not been provided. They asked the hotel manager for one, but were answered with a head-shake. Then the Queen's dresser spotted a long mirror on the wall of the ladies' loo. Between them, the page and footman took it down, carried it to the Queen's room, up-ended it and propped it into position with a pile of books.

A miniature mountain of luggage accompanies the Queen wherever she goes. Two large travelling wardrobes hold her coats and dresses. Six feet high, covered in blue leather, they are mounted on wheels to make for easier handling. Also on wheels is the matching leather-covered chest of drawers which the Queen had specially made for her world travels. In it are her gloves, handkerchiefs, underwear and so on. There are hat and shoe boxes also in blue leather. Large leather trunks contain the clothes she will not need until later in the trip. The state gown, if she has one along, requires a trunk all to itself to avoid creasing. A crocodile dressing case holds the thirty-piece set of silver gilt brushes, combs, mirrors and cosmetic jars which was one of her wedding gifts. A long slender case, handed down from Queen Mary, holds umbrellas and sunshades, each in its individual dust-cover.

With her on her travels the Queen always takes her own pillows (to help her sleep better), a hot water bottle (in case it is chilly at night), a supply of Malvern water (as a precaution against tummy upsets), a canister of her favourite tea, her own toilet soap, some of her favourite chocolate-covered mints, a supply of barley sugar (as an antidote against possible travel sickness) and a batch of crossword puzzles.

There was an occasion, just before the Queen was due at the White House in Washington, when the canister of tea went astray. Knowing that the first thing she would want would be a cup of tea, one of her staff dashed along to the presidential kitchen. But all they had there were tea-bags and an experimental brew-up looked rather too weak for the royal palate. It does not seem to have occurred to anyone simply to open the tea-bags and pour out the contents. Instead, there was another frantic search until a solitary quarter-pound packet of tea was finally unearthed to keep the royal teapot going until the Queen's own tea came to light again.

Wherever she goes, the Queen takes her cameras with her. She is an enthusiastic photographer and the amateur movies she has taken over the years are perhaps the modern equivalent of the journals Queen Victoria kept so assiduously. From her perch in the fig tree she was filming baboons, rhino and water buck on the day she became Queen. Over the years since she has filmed Everest from the air, the armada of small boats which greeted her in Sydney and the spouting jets of the fire boats which welcomed her to New York. She has filmed a tiger hunt, a crocodile shoot, shark fishing and porpoises undulating in the wake of the royal yacht. She has filmed horse racing in Britain and elephants hauling teak logs in Thailand. She has films of the Taj Mahal, the hot springs at Rotorua in New Zealand, the fall in Canada and the Equestrian Olympic Games in Sweden. She has filmed the ceremony of Buddha's Tooth in Sri Lanka and the apes at Gibraltar. She also has an hilarious sequence of Philip in a butcher's apron, his nose reddened with grease-paint, taking part in the crossing-the-line ceremony during their round the world trip of 1953-4.

On one trip to America she took three cameras with her in a zip-fastened hold-all. When the zip-fastener broke, one of her staff tied the hold-all with string as a temporary measure. U.S. security men, spotting the string as the hold-all was being taken aboard the royal plane, could perhaps be excused for not believing that it belonged to the Queen. They insisted on carrying it well clear of the aircraft and checking it for a possible bomb.

But the panic on that occasion was short-lived compared with what ensued when the Queen's jewels went missing in New Zealand. The Queen knew nothing of it at the time; she had already left for Wellington when the loss was discovered. The hotel at which she had stayed overnight was hastily searched from top to bottom, without result. Then someone came up with the thought that troops helping with the rest of the royal baggage had perhaps taken the royal jewel-case by mistake.

Members of the Queen's staff piled into a car and drove in pursuit, arriving at the local airport only to find that that the rest of the baggage was already airborne. They commandeered another plane and continued the chase. Landing at Wellington, they found that the baggage plane had already been unloaded and its contents were now on their way to Government House. Another car, another chase, and one can imagine with what huge sighs of relief they finally caught up with the missing jewel-case— standing unguarded on the front steps of Government House.

Voluminous though the Queen's own luggage is, it forms only part of the baggage which is shipped around on a state visit or royal tour. For the Queen's 1972 state visit to France, the advance luggage alone weighed almost a ton. It included a dinner service bearing Queen Victoria's cypher and a gold Georgian cutlery set for use when the Queen entertained President Pompidou at the British embassy. Six tons of stuff were choppered ashore from the royal yacht for her 1975 visit to Mexico. And a staggering twelve tons was manhandled around during the 1953-4 world tour.

Visiting France in 1972, the Queen also took Madame Pompidou some books for her grandchildren. Wherever the Queen goes, she must take along gifts to be distributed as her visit progresses, medals and orders, gold cufflinks and jewelled brooches, signed photographs and powder compacts embossed with her royal cypher, something as a thank-you for everyone from the head of state she is visiting down to butlers and maids, cooks and chauffeurs. As in the case of Madame Pompidou she tries to ensure that the gifts suit the recipient, even to the extent, on one visit to the United States, of taking the late President Eisenhower a coffee table inlaid with a map of the D-Day invasion beaches.

Invariably, there are other gifts to be brought back when she returns home. She returned from one tour of Canada with 120 gifts, from a gold and silver desk set to a pair of bead gloves made by the Blackfoot Indians. On one visit to the United States she was given a gold-plated model of the Empire State Building, a pair of eighteenth-century riding spurs, a replica of George Washington's riding crop and a mink coat, to mention only a few things. In France she was given a Renault car, a Louis Quinze clock, the largest bottle of perfume ever made and the smallest watch, a replica of one she had lost.

She returned from her world tour with over four hundred gifts, ranging from nylon nightdresses to a century-old tortoise egg. In Ghana she was given lionskins and leopard skins, elephant tusks and a gold model of a chief's palanquin (a cross between a throne and a sedan chair). In Nigeria there were fans and native furniture, shawls and turbans, and a paperweight made from a tiger's paw. From Brazil she came back with a gold model of Brasilia cathedral, the gold key of Sao Paulo, a tiara, an emerald bracelet, a coffee service, miscellaneous gold medallions, several paintings and a cup carved out of rhino horn.

Wherever the Queen goes, an entourage of some thirty people goes with her. To Japan in 1975 she took along the Lord Privy Seal, two ladies-in-waiting, her Private Secretary, an Assistant Private Secretary, her Press Secretary, a physician, the Captain of the Queen's Flight and an equerry. In addition she had with her a detective or two, a hairdresser, two dressers, six footmen, two maids and four clerks. Philip, accompanying her, will usually have with him his Private Secretary, an equerry, a detective and at least one of his two valets.

It is sometimes a good thing the Queen does have her own servants along with her. There was one overseas lunch when,

Time off on the farm at
Balmoral

On a visit to Rothes
Colliery, Kircaldy

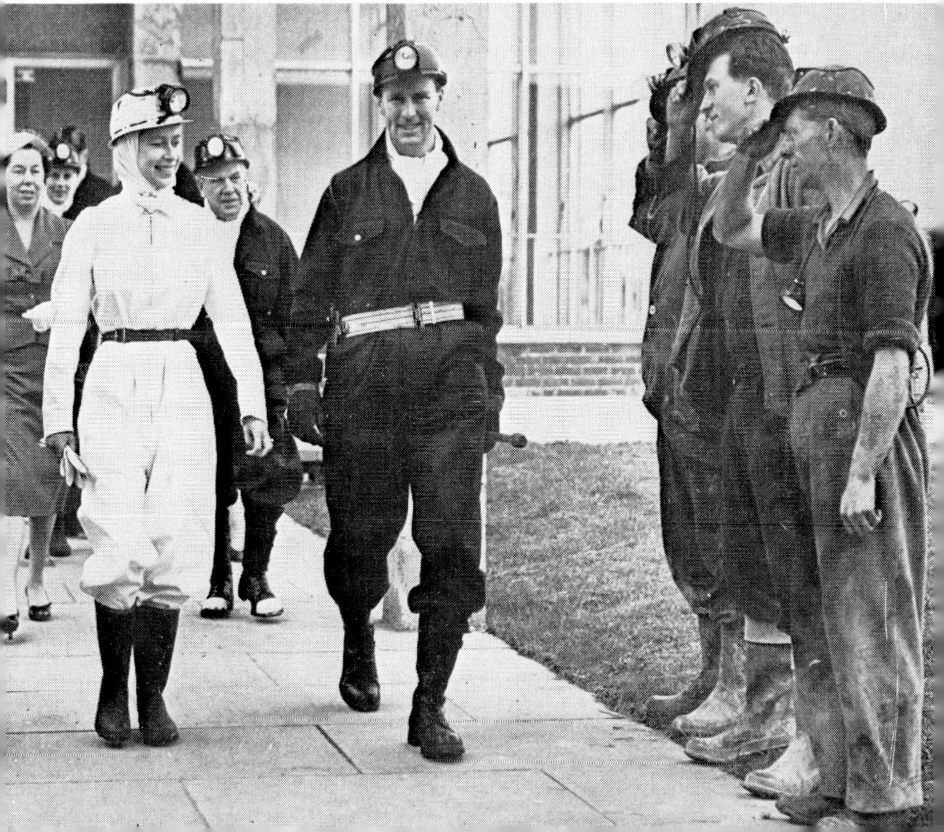

Royalty and De Gaulle go to the ballet

The Queen, surrounded by Ghanaians, on the tour of 1961

otherwise, she would perhaps not have got anything to eat. The local waitresses who were supposed to be serving her were reduced to such a state of nerves they could not go anywhere near her. Fortunately, the Queen's page spotted what was happening and he and a footman took over.

But sometimes, on the other hand, the fact that the Queen takes along her own staff can lead to confusion. At one place where the Queen was due to stay, it was discovered, at almost the last moment, that the royal bed had not been made. The resident housekeeper was summoned.

" It's not my job," she protested. " I'm the housekeeper, not a housemaid. I thought Her Majesty would be bringing her own maid."

She looked rather pointedly at Margaret Macdonald as she said it.

" And I," said Miss Macdonald, " am the Queen's Dresser."

We do not know which of them made the royal bed in the end, but someone did.

H

7

Royal Consort

With his thinning thatch and the need to wear glasses when at
the wheel of his car (though he usually keeps them out of sight
until he is clear of the crowds), with his polo-playing days firmly
behind him, it would be idle to pretend that Philip is still the
young Greek god of a prince he was in the days when his wife
first succeeded to the throne. But he is still lean and athletic in
his fifties, as active as ever, driving, flying and choppering about
Britain and the world at large, a complex mixture of princely
charm and ducal arrogance, both a man's man and a woman's
man.

He is perhaps most at ease in the all-male atmosphere of a
ship's bridge or the flight deck of an aircraft. Yet, without in any
way contriving it, he continues to radiate the sexuality of a regal
pop-star. It is a knack he has always had. Years ago, accompanying his wife on their round-the-world tour, close observers
pondered why it was, wherever the pair of them went, there were
invariably more girls on one side of the royal route then the other.
Then the answer dawned on them. That was the side Philip sat.

There was also the occasion when officers' wives at a U.S. air
base took as their subject for monthly debate the lighthearted
question of whether or not they would like to be Queen Elizabeth
II. One attractive young matron was perhaps speaking for more
than herself when she said that Yes, she would, and gave her
reason in three words: " That Prince Philip. . . ."

As with the Queen, it is impossible (because there is no basis
for exact calculation) to assess what Philip has achieved over the
years of his wife's monarchy. Unfortunately for Britain, his ex-
hortations to pull digits out and forget the old adage that " British
is best " appear to have gone largely unheeded. If he is remem-

bered for anything in the years ahead, it will perhaps be—and he would perhaps wish it to be—for his Duke of Edinburgh Award Scheme which he originally conceived and pioneered around twenty years ago.

Philip can perhaps explain the scheme better than we could, as he does in an introduction to the official handbook: " Young people growing up in an industrial society have many difficulties to face and not many opportunities for personal achievements . . . This scheme is intended to help both the young and those who take an interest in their welfare. It is designed as an introduction to leisure time activities, a challenge to the individual to personal achievement, and as a guide to those people and organizations who are concerned about the development of our future citizens."

It is in brief, a scheme to channel the energies and enthusiasms of the young into a challenging programme of activities. The tangible targets are Olympics-style awards—golds, silvers and bronzes. The real objectives, even if the youngsters themselves are often unaware of the fact, are the development of maturity and responsibility.

Of the more than seven thousand boys who took part in the first year of the scheme's inception, more than one thousand qualified for silver and bronze awards. The following year there were 8,530 new entrants and the number of award winners rose to 2,584, including eighty-two golds. Girls were admitted to the scheme in 1959 and by 1961 it was also making its presence felt overseas. Youngsters were now coming forward at a rate of over 60,000 a year. The climb continued, with slight falls here and there along the way, until the 1972-4 period saw new entrants totalling over 90,000 each year. By the end of 1974 a total of well over a million youngsters had taken part in the scheme, nearly half of whom had gained awards—37,127 golds, 113,182 silvers and 273,357 bronzes. As well as Britain, it was operating now in some twenty-five Commonwealth countries, from Canada to the Falkland Isles, from New Zealand to Bermuda. No wonder Philip could say, with truth and perhaps a small degree of pardonable pride: " It has probably done more for people than anything else I have been involved in."

Each year, to maintain interest in the scheme, he carries out two tours. In 1972, for instance, during two crowded days in Cheshire and Lancashire, he met or saw some seven thousand young people taking part in the scheme. On a second tour that year, of Oxfordshire and Berkshire, he saw, among other things, one group of youngsters manipulating a hot-air balloon and another group bathing a three-week-old baby. In 1973, he toured Lincolnshire, Rutland, Leicestershire and Northamptonshire, attended the Australian Pacific Conference and visited nineteen centres in Queensland, New South Wales, Victoria, Tasmania, South and Western Australia. In 1974 he again toured Berkshire as well as Buckinghamshire, Bedfordshire, Hertfordshire, Essex and, later in the year, West Yorkshire.

And each year he receives those who gain their golds at either Buckingham Palace or Holyroodhouse. Several hundred youngsters attend each presentation. They are divided into small groups and Philip goes round, chatting to each group in turn as he hands out certificates in small bundles for individual presentation.

Others of the Royal Family help out with the presentation of awards from time to time. In 1973 the Duchess of Kent presented golds at the headquarters of the Milton Keynes Development Corporation. The same year the Queen presented golds at Charlottetown in Prince Edward Island (while Philip did the same in Ottawa) and the following year the Queen Mother, on a visit to Canada, presented golds in Toronto. But the mainspring of the scheme is, and has always been, Philip himself.

His interest in young people is no artificial culture. It is part of the man himself, that same combination of qualities which has made him a good father to his children, consistently encouraging them along the right paths without ever coercing them. In particular, he has encouraged them to do things ahead of their years. Charles and Anne, for instance, were both driving Land Rovers about the private roads of the royal Balmoral estate well before they were of an age to be legally permitted to drive on what is known as the Queen's highway. Philip's view is that youngsters enjoy learning things early. " Later on," he says, " there is a sense of embarrassment at being a beginner."

Equally, he has encouraged his own children to take the " calculated risks " which he believes are essential to the growing-up process, though ensuring always, of course, that they have been both properly trained and are properly supervised.

" Proper training removes most of the hazards in what, to the uninitiated, look like dangerous activities," he has said. " The risk comes from letting children do things under the guidance of ignorant or incompetent adults and without proper training and preparation. The real danger is ignorance."

As a husband too, he has been consistently encouraging and protective, bolstering the Queen with some witty aside if she has seemed in danger of succumbing to nerves on a public occasion, bridging the gap with a quick quip when she has dried up in conversation with strangers, and even sometimes losing his temper when he thought too much was being demanded of her. It was Philip's idea, some years back, that the Queen should tape-record her speeches in advance and listen to the playback, as he did himself. Her better projection on public occasions dates from that time.

Whatever other criticisms may have been levelled against him over the years, and there have been many, few will deny that Philip is, and has always been, a hard worker. Even Willie Hamilton has paid him the somewhat doubtful compliment of saying that he is the only Royal who really works for his money (which seems rather unfair to the Queen, who also works hard though perhaps less obviously).

In his fifties, Philip still works as hard as ever. An average working day can run to thirteen hours; eighteen hours is not unknown. There was one tour of South America when, in forty-four days, he attended fifty receptions, twenty-two dinners and twelve luncheons, laid eleven wreaths and one foundation stone, paid sixty-eight visits to factories, mines, plantations, schools and churches, and made thirty speeches.

After a full working day, culminating with an evening engagement, he will often sit signing letters or drafting another speech in his gadget-filled study when it would perhaps be better if he was in bed. The strain sometimes shows in his face. Behind his back, royal servants refer to it as his " Annigoni look ", an expression stemming from the grim, non-smiling portrait Annigoni once painted of him.

When he shows signs of wear and tear, his aides do their best to curb him. It is, as the Queen herself found out years ago, a well-nigh hopeless task. " If he takes on much more," she remarked once, " he soon won't have time for breakfast."

Philip may still find time for breakfast, but not infrequently it is a hurried, gobbled meal. To Philip, meals are necessary but frustrating breaks, like stopping the car to fill up with petrol on a long journey. "He'd be much happier if he could simply swallow a couple of pills and carry straight on working," a former royal servant says of him.

Even a minor bout of ill-health cannot always persuade him to apply the necessary brakes. There was a Sunday at Windsor when he went down with what looked suspiciously like flu. The Queen persuaded him to go to bed and sent for a doctor.

The doctor examined him, told him to stay in bed and said that he would look in again the following day.

If he did, he was wasting his time. Though still running a temperature, Philip was up as usual the following morning to drive himself back to London. Work came first.

Philip has been fortunate in that his health has been basically good over the years. Which has been fortunate also for those around him. Even minor ailments make him so frustrated and irritable that he is " almost unbearable "—or so his wife supposedly said on one occasion. But healthy, athletic and energetic though he has always been, he cannot now escape altogether the sort of ailments which overtake many active men in their middle years, like the recurring wrist condition which compelled him to give up polo in the same year in which he celebrated his fiftieth birthday.

Being Philip, he immediately substituted something else of course : coaching (or four-in-hand driving, as it is sometimes called). And being Philip, he continued to display the same dash and daring with the reins as he had previously shown on the polo field. And sometimes with the same unfortunate results, as when he was kicked by one of his horses after his wagonette over-turned.

Looking at Philip today, always on the go, both " First Gentleman " of the realm and very much a man-of-the-people when he wants to be, it is difficult to realize that there was a time, at the outset of his wife's reign, when he had too little to do and felt considerably out of things. He is supposed to have said at the time that he was no more than " a lodger " at Buckingham Palace. Whether he actually said it or not, that was certainly how he felt. He had sacrificed a promising naval career to be at his young wife's side as she deputized more and more for her sick father. Then came the death of her father and her own accession to the throne. Now it was to those who had been her father's advisers that she necessarily turned for guidance and Philip felt himself elbowed out. For the Queen, in those early days of monarchy, there was almost too much to do. For Philip, there was too little.

There was, as he quickly found out, no proper provision in Britain's system of constitutional monarchy for the husband of a Queen. The wife of a King would automatically have become Queen on her husband's accession, with all a Queen's privileges and responsibilities. For instance, a Queen would have shared the King's immunity from tax. But the husband of a Queen does not become King, does not share her immunity from tax, has few privileges and no responsibilities. And Philip is a man to whom responsibility is virtually a necessity.

In those early days, he had to stand by while his children became Windsors instead of Mountbattens. He was not—still is not—permitted to be present when his wife received the prime minister in audience. He was not—is not—permitted to see the contents of the sacred boxes. Queen Victoria's husband, Albert, may have done so, but not Philip. In Albert's day, there was no such post as Private Secretary to the Queen. Or if there was, the holder of it was a mere copier of letters, a sort of overgrown messenger boy. Albert very quickly elevated himself to the position of unofficial Private Secretary. And more. He even drafted out the replies his wife sent to the prime minister, the foreign secretary and others. But by the time Victoria's great-great-grand-daughter succeeded to the throne, things had changed a great deal. Elizabeth II does not have anything like the political influence and power Queen Victoria wielded so autocratically and so effectively. So Philip could not hope to be a second Albert even if he wished. In fact, he did not. While he read up a great deal about the Prince Consort, it was perhaps more with a view to avoiding pitfalls than with the idea of emulation.

Yet he may have observed that they had some things in common. Both were the products of an unsettled upbringing; both could become quickly irritated when things did not go their way. But there the similarities ended. Albert was stiff, unbending and pedantic, an introverted idealist and intellectual who was never properly understood by his wife's subjects. Philip is an extrovert, a man of action rather than an intellectual, with the ability to unbend, though perhaps only at times and places of his own choosing.

Philip is too intelligent not to have foreseen that he would necessarily have to take something of a back seat when his wife became Queen. But he had perhaps not banked upon it happening so soon in their married life; before he had had sufficient time to establish himself in his own right. As a result, he found himself, for a time, with no proper job of work. A few crumbs came his way, like helping to select the designs for stamps and coins for the new reign, but these can have been of small comfort to a man who once had the responsibility of commanding his own naval frigate. His frustration showed sometimes in bouts of gloom which one would not normally associate with his active, extrovert nature.

In those early days he already held a few official appointments, but not enough for a young man of his energy and ability. To fill his time, he inspected Buckingham Palace from top to bottom and came up with various ideas for reorganization. One idea was that the palace should install its own laundry and so reduce the bills for outside laundering. But the palace belongs to the nation, not the Queen, and the custodians of the nation's finances vetoed the idea because of the capital outlay involved.

Even in small things, Philip found that he could not do as he wished. In an endeavour to brighten up the corridor outside the royal apartment, he had a particular painting moved there from another part of the palace. This time it was the Queen herself who vetoed the change.

" That painting belongs to the state," she said. " We can't move those." And back the painting had to go.

But if Buckingham Palace belonged to the nation, Sandringham was his wife's private property. Philip moved in and reorganized things so that the estate there became less of a drain on the royal purse than it had been in the days of the Queen's father.

He also fulfilled a long-held ambition by learning to fly. Back in his Gordonstoun days he had debated whether to go into the Navy or the Air Force and had been finally persuaded into the Navy by his Uncle Dickie (Earl Mountbatten of Burma). But even in the matter of flying lessons he found himself battling official objections every step of the way. After his first six months' training, for instance, he found he could not move on to the next stage, night flying, until the matter had been referred all the way up to the prime minister.

Bit by bit, he won the battle, qualifying as a pilot in 1953 and converting to helicopters three years later. Over the years since, flying has become an indispensable part of his way of life. Without it, he would be quite unable to cope with anything like the number of public engagements he undertakes. There was one particularly hectic spell in 1963-4 when he visited twenty-five countries in nine months, and still found time to take Charles and Anne on a continental ski-ing jaunt during their winter holiday. There was another occasion, a three-week tour of Canada involving twenty-five take-offs and landings, when he was at the aircraft controls for over sixty hours, while during a ten-day, 36,000-mile tour of South America he did the flying himself for just under a hundred hours.

But in those early days of monarchy, flying was only a hobby and Sandringham a sideline. Neither could fill the void created by his resignation from the Navy. At one time Philip had hoped that he would one day return to the sea. But now that his wife was Queen there was clearly no likelihood of that. A man of different type, making the best of a bad job, might very easily have settled for a life of lotus-eating indolence and no one in those days could legitimately have complained had Philip adopted this course. In fact, some might have preferred it, happier not to have Philip putting his spoke in.

But indolence is not in Philip's nature and gradually over the next few years he was to create his own orbit of royal interests and princely duties. He concentrated particularly on those areas in which the Queen, being a woman, might perhaps not have overmuch interest—science, industry and sport. Youth and education too.

" I haven't got a job," Philip said once. " I'm self-employed."

In a sense, that is true. And self-employment has also been self-created.

Over the years the number of his official appointments was to increase at a prodigious pace and requests for him to go here, there and everywhere were presently streaming in at a rate of over a hundred a month. However willing a work-horse he might be, no man could possibly accept them all. Philip's reaction was to fit in as many as possible on a first-come-first-served basis.

Today he adopts a rather more businesslike approach. Incoming requests are salted away for a period of six months, then sorted out, considered and decided upon so that he shares himself out more fairly. Of the up to six hundred requests he receives each half-year, he manages to accept about twenty-five per cent. Because there are also public engagements he must necessarily attend with the Queen, it can mean some pretty tight scheduling.

There was a day in 1974 when he attended an 11.30 a.m. service with the Queen at St. Paul's and joined her again at 6.15 p.m. at a reception for Commonwealth officials. In between he had lunch with the board of I.C.I. and then took the chair at a meeting of the Zoological Society. And in the evening, after the reception, he dashed off to the Connaught Rooms to have dinner with the English-Speaking Union. The following day he presented the Design Council awards before joining the Queen at a reception given by the King George Jubilee Trust. That evening he attended the 150th anniversary dinner of the Athenaeum Club and the next day he was off to Salford.

For Philip, five engagements in a day is by no means unusual. Fairly typical was the day on which he opened a conference at 9.30, lunched with the Grand Order of Water Rats at 12.30, presided over a meeting of the World Wildlife Fund at 3, went on to attend a meeting of the Wildfowl Trust at 4.30 and ended the day at a six o'clock lecture with dinner to follow. In the course of an average working year he will carry out 250-300 engagements in his own right (apart from those he attends with the Queen), travelling perhaps 75,000 miles and making around eighty speeches, many of which never find their way into the national newspapers. He defines his work as "responding to demand; trying to react to what people expect."

While much of the planning and preparation is necessarily delegated to his staff (small compared with that of the Queen), his speeches are always his own work and his fertile brain will often toss into the pool an imaginative idea to provide the novel touch. As with the request, some years ago, to inaugurate a Prince Philip Greyhound Trophy. Most men would have settled for the traditional silver cup. The idea of a silver dog collar was Philip's own. So, incidentally, was the idea for putting a selection of royal art on show to the public in the Queen's Gallery at Buckingham Palace.

It was in 1956, the year in which he also launched his Award Scheme, that Philip's globe-trotting really began. It started with an invitation to open the Olympic Games, held that year in Australia. Philip looked at his maps and came up with the idea of also visiting some of the places and people the Queen, as a woman, might find it more difficult to visit. The result was to combine with the Australian trip visits to the trans-Antarctic expedition, the Falkland Isles and other isolated outposts of Britain's dwindling empire. There have been not a few similar expeditions over the years since.* So much so that sometimes he has seemed to be spending more time abroad than in Britain.

Over the years of monarchy Philip has consistently seemed the most controversial member of the Royal Family. Daughter Anne may occasionally have surpassed him in the field, but not often and not for long. That Philip has so often found himself the subject of critical headlines has not always been his fault. As Anne pointed out on one occasion, any long-running serial needs a baddie to offset the goodies, and the Royal Family saga is no exception. The Queen is clearly the goody. So Philip, like it or not, has not infrequently found himself cast as the baddie.

True, it has sometimes seemed as though he has set out to grab that particular role. The Queen, thanks to her long years of early training, consistently conforms, projecting the right sort of public image (or what she and her advisers think is the right sort of public image). She does what is expected of her; says what is expected of her. She does not indulge in witty repartee which can sometimes misfire. Her speeches, while often dull, are undeniably safe.

But Philip did not have the same early training as his wife. Nor is it in his nature to play it safe all the time.

Ever since Coronation year, when he got into hot water for advocating the character-building advantages of conscription, he has found himself classed as " a royal meddler " on and off. He has upset newspaper editors (he once called the *Daily Express* " a bloody awful newspaper ") and interviewers (as when he told an American commentator to " stuff " his microphone), politicians and businessmen. He even upset Britain's Government of the day with his comment that " We live in the most regimented society

* Appendix IV.

ever in this country." Many people agreed with him!

Some of his other remarks over the years have been less extensively reported and are less well remembered. To quote one : " I see no advantage in a prosperous and powerful state if it is to be achieved at the expense of human freedom and happiness." And another : " All people are primarily citizens and not just workers with a bit of private life."

Philip has been described to us as having the ability " to strip off the outer layers and see through to the core of a problem." Certainly there have been times when he has seemed to see things more clearly than most . . . and further ahead. As far back as 1971 he was comparing Britain to " a man living beyond his means."

Philip himself once said that speeches should primarily be " safe ", adding that, " People would rather be bored than offended." His track record shows that he has not always practised what he preaches. Sometimes, clearly, he has meant what he has said, however controversial, and has stood by it during the furore which followed. But there have been other times when he has been misunderstood or quoted out of context or when what he probably intended as a joke was taken the wrong way.

There was, for instance, the occasion when, visiting Calgary, he was presented with the traditional white stetson by the local mayor.

" What, another?" said Philip. " Well, I suppose I can use it as a flower pot."

A joke? Of course. But some people took it the wrong way, the mayor among them. However, he managed to get his own back a day or so later when making another presentation to Philip. This time it was a pair of horns with a seven-foot spread.

" Don't ask me what to do with it and I won't tell you where to stick it," he informed Philip.

In his schooldays Philip was once described as " intolerant and impatient." He still is. He does not suffer those he regards as fools gladly. It irritates him when arrangements go wrong. Stupid things done in the name of monarchy sometimes irritate and sometimes amuse him. It angers him if he feels the Queen is being imposed on. He becomes fidgety if interviewers ask what he considers to be stupid questions. On his side, he usually familiarizes himself sufficiently with a subject to ask the right questions.

" He doesn't know a great deal about science, but he knows enough to ask sensible questions," an American scientist said of him after the two of them had met in San Francisco.

Philip once said that he could read about himself in a newspaper with the same detachment " that I read about some animal in the Zoo." While he may believe that to be true, the evidence is to the contrary. He is a much more sensitive man than appears on the surface and newspaper criticisms of himself, his wife or his children disturb him more than he would perhaps care to admit.

Gibes at the monarchy or sneers at the Commonwealth can equally infuriate him. He was particularly incensed when he arrived in America with the Queen to be confronted by Malcolm Muggeridge's article in the *Saturday Evening Post* entitled: " Does Britain Really Need A Queen?"

" If they must print this rubbish, does it have to be while we are here?" he demanded, tetchily.

Philip himself believes passionately in both the monarchy and the Commonwealth. " There are some things for which it is worthwhile making some personal sacrifice and I believe that the Commonwealth is one of those things," he said on one occasion.

And on another, in a speech directed specifically at Australia and New Zealand: " If ever our friends find themselves in difficulties, then there are a goodly number of people in this country who will overcome any obstacle to go to their assistance."

Over the years Philip has acquired a reputation for being arrogant, sarcastic, impatient and quick-tempered and undoubtedly he can be all these things at times. He can be a distinct joker at times and places of his own choosing, but his jokes, often, have a bite to them.

In Borneo, in 1972, when a local warrior, despite much huffing and puffing, was quite unable to launch a dart from his blowpipe, Philip remarked, grinning, " It's probably full of fluff."

Even Anne, on that occasion, was moved to chide him: " That's unkind."

But there is, as of course there must be, another side to the princely coin. Like the Queen Mother, he can sustain his quizzical smile and an apparent show of interest in the most humdrum things for a long time if he is in the right mood. In the right mood too, he can be understanding, thoughtful, helpful.

If winners of his Duke of Edinburgh awards, unnerved or

over-excited by the occasion, forget to shake hands with him, he
is quick to thrust out his own hand. If others laughed when a
woman overbalanced while curtsying to him in Australia, Philip
did not. He scowled at those who laughed and subsequently
sought out the woman to chat with her and relieve her embarrassment.

And it was Philip who stopped, after several other motorists
had passed by on the other side, to help a caravaner whose car
had broken down near Balmoral. He ordered his Land-Rover
round so that car and caravan could be towed out of the way.

Assessing Philip's character at the time he applied to go into
the Navy, his old headmaster at Gordonstoun, Dr Kurt Hahn,
wrote as follows : " Prince Philip is a born leader, but will need
the exacting demands of a great service to do justice to himself.
His best is outstanding; his second best is not good enough."

That was over thirty years ago and it is intriguing, all these
years later, to speculate whether his role as the Queen's husband
has enabled Philip to give of his " outstanding " best. That he
has done all and more than has been required of him is undeniable. But how much more might he have done had it been
demanded ? While Philip himself may not realize it, the tragedy
is that, because he is who he is, his " outstanding " best has had
to be restricted to relatively minor spheres, like the Award Scheme.
Judging by the way he has caused that to grow and mature, what
might the man not have done in some really worthwhile position
of political or naval responsibility?

There have been times when he has seemed to be acting as
cheer-leader from the sidelines, but too often his has been the
voice of a prophet crying in the wilderness. Too often his comments have been met with criticism when they should have been
greeted with applause. He has had more than his fair quota of
mud slung at him over the years. Indeed, there was a brief period
in 1969 when there was so much mud flying in his direction that
it seemed he might vanish from sight under it all.

It started in Ottawa with his challenging remark that " We
(the Royals) do not come here for the benefit of our health."
Uproar in Canada. Further uproar in Britain—and questions in
Parliament—when word filtered through that he had made some
fairly startling revelations about royal finances on American
television. His suggestion that he and the Queen might find them-

selves moving into smaller premises was surely a joke (though at Sandringham, since, they have actually done so). But underlying the princely quip was the hard financial fact: "We have kept the whole thing (monarchy) going on a budget based on the costs of eighteen years ago."

A second American television interview made further big headlines back home. Philip had been asked about the possibility that the Queen might abdicate.

"It has its attractions," was his first quick comment—another joke, surely—followed immediately by: "I don't think it has been thought of very seriously."

Maybe not, but his comments put Britain's newspapers in such a state of tizzy that you might have thought the Queen was seriously contemplating following in Uncle David's footsteps.

As if all this was not enough, hardly was Philip back home than he found himself embroiled in the business of Tom Jones. What Philip actually said after hearing Jones the Voice in action at the Royal Variety Show is perhaps a matter of interpretation. Philip's own recollection, we understand, is that his remarks were intended to indicate that he did not think much of the choice of songs. Others thought he was saying he did not think much of Tom's singing and that, at least initially, was how it emerged in the headlines.

In the further *brouhaha* which followed it was left to an American to come to Philip's rescue. A New Yorker, writing an open letter to the British people (via the *Daily Express*) had this to say: "Do you not appreciate that this man of extraordinary intellect and articulation does more to uphold everything we like and admire about Britain than a whole army of politicians and pressmen? It is against your own interest to make it so uncomfortable for the Duke that you effectively muzzle him on future trips abroad."

For a time it seemed that Philip had indeed been muzzled. Perhaps he had had as much controversy and criticism as he could take at the time. Perhaps, far-sighted as he has sometimes shown himself to be, he realized that Britain was entering an era when monarchy must walk a yet trickier tightrope. And perhaps it was merely that the public spotlight tended to swing away from him for a time and focus instead on son Charles.

But as this book is being written, he would seem to be in good voice again. He has had his say against those who bleat about the cost of Concorde. He has had something to say about the " parasites of agriculture ", subsequently assuring the 15,000-strong staff of the Agricultural Development and Advisory Service that he did not mean them. And risking what he called " the barbed wire entanglements of political and economic dogma . . . a sacred C.B.I. cow . . . a tender union corn . . . a party political booby trap," he was again trying to point the way ahead to a depressed and apathetic Britain.

" Controls, restrictions and limitations do nothing but inhibit change and discourage enterprise . . . You can always find someone to praise for a success or a culprit to blame for a wrong decision, but it's almost impossible to identify those responsible for the consequences of doing nothing until it is much too late.

" The dead hand of the No-men has an even more sinister consequence . . . It starts by being a restriction on the other fellow, but experience and history have shown that a restriction on one section of the community has a way of growing into restrictions on all sections of the community.

" Freedom is not simply a matter of freedom of speech. It is also freedom to do and that can only flourish under a liberal law. It is destroyed under arbitrary control or by anarchy just as effectively as freedom of speech is by censorship."

By the time this book is published, we shall perhaps just see whether or not his words have been heeded.

8

Heir to the Throne

A royal page named Stanley Childs was first with the news when the future Queen Elizabeth II, married a little less than a year and (if she could have foreseen the future) only a little more than three years removed from monarchy, gave birth to her first child on 14th November 1948. One or two others, including the baby's father, Prince Philip, fresh from the squash court and a cooling dip in the palace pool, may have had the news minutes earlier, but it was an excited Childs who slipped out of Buckingham Palace, ran across the forecourt and yelled "It's a boy" to the waiting crowd outside the palace railings.

Shortly afterwards an official bulletin corrected this unofficial announcement. According to the bulletin, the then Princess Elizabeth, Duchess of Edinburgh, had been "safely delivered" of a "Prince".

Prince or boy, the birth was not witnessed by a Government minister charged with the task of ensuring that no changeling was introduced into the royal line. Ahead of the baby's birth, the royal grandfather, King George VI, mindful of the fiasco which had attended the birth of his own daughter Margaret, when the Home Secretary of the day sat kicking his heels for two weeks and then arrived on the scene too late to witness anything, had finally ended the anachronistic custom on the grounds that it was neither a statutory requirement nor a constitutional necessity.

The baby was christened Charles Philip Arthur George. Charles because his parents liked the name, Philip after his father and George after his grandfather. Arthur was a bit of a puzzler and one expert on royal names hazarded an opinion that it was a link with Queen Victoria's son, Arthur, Duke of Connaught, who had died seven years earlier at the ripe old age of ninety-one.

I

Be that as it may, Charles Philip Arthur George from birth was second in the line of succession, though it was not until after his grandfather's death and almost on the eve of his mother's coronation that he received his first inkling of his future destiny. Even then, it came not from his parents but from a servant.

He was trotting along one of the palace corridors when he came across a footman brushing the long robe of royal purple which the Queen would wear after her crowning. Boy-like inquisitiveness caused him to stop and ask what was going on. The man explained that the robe was being prepared for the Queen.

" Who is the Queen ? " was the boy's next question.

" Your Mummy, of course."

He was only four at the time and, following his grandfather's death, now next in the line of succession.* His mother, because of the possibility that her parents might one day have a son to take precedence over her, had been only Heiress Presumptive when her father was on the throne. But Charles, as a first-born boy, was now Heir Apparent, yielding precedence to no one. It was time for his training to start and his grandmother, the widowed Queen Mother, had him with her in Westminster Abbey to watch part of his mother's coronation, though he was perhaps more interested in a new dressing which had been used on his hair. He smoothed his hair with his hand, sniffed his hand and held it out towards his grandmother.

" Smell, Granny."

And somewhere around this time, judging by an overheard conversation he had with his small sister, Princess Anne, his destiny was explained to him in simple terms. The two children were watching the changing of the guard from one of the palace windows. Anne thought it was " a coronation ", but Charles knew better.

" There won't be another coronation for years and years," he told her. " And that will be mine."

Charles himself has said since that he does not remember the incident, but we have it on good authority.

His early childhood, like that of his mother before him, was warm and secure; cosseted. Too cosseted, his father was perhaps inclined to think. On all sides he was hemmed in by protective

* Appendix II.

femininity, his mother and nanny and a governess who came later. And there was Granny, the Queen Mother, to look after him when his parents were away on a royal tour or state visit. His only links with the male world were his father, who gave him swimming lessons, the groom who taught him to ride, and the young footman who fetched and carried in the royal nursery.

For lessons with his governess he was the only child in a class of one. Though his name had been provisionally put down for Eton almost at birth, it is debatable whether his mother would have sent him to school at all had the decision been left entirely to her. After all, she had never been to school herself. Nor had her parents before her. But her husband had been to school. In fact, to a variety of schools, in France, England, Germany and Scotland. Moreover, he had both enjoyed his schooldays and, he felt, benefited from them. Father-like, he wanted his son to do the same.

Philip's wishes were to bring about a big change in the traditional pattern of royal upbringing. Charles's dancing lessons came to an abrupt halt. Even music lessons, for a time, were curtailed. Instead, he was sent out to play football with other boys, trot round a running track and exercise in a gymnasium. The services of nanny Helen Lightbody were dispensed with and she was retired to a grace-and-favour apartment. Charles himself was sorry to see her go. In many ways she had been like a second mother to him. So strong was the bond between them that years later, as a young man, he would call in from time to time at her home near the Oval cricket ground to see how she was and he even arranged for her to journey to Caernarvon to witness his installation as Prince of Wales.

When it was first announced that Charles was going to school, some people were inclined to give the credit to the then Lord Altrincham and his highly critical article on royal upbringing in the *National & English Review*. In fact, the royal parents had already made their decision before the article was published. Not, it is true, to let the future King mix with potential dockers and bus-drivers, as the article advocated, but at least to send him to his father's old school, Cheam.

It was, by royal standards, a bold experiment from which the Queen's two younger sons, Andrew and Edward, have benefited. Charles himself was to benefit too in the long run. But to do so, he had first to endure what his mother, looking back, realizes were "terrible times" for one so young. Wherever he went in those days of boyhood he was dogged by photographers, trailed by reporters, surrounded by sightseers. There were stories about him in the newspapers on sixty-eight of the eighty-eight days of his first term at Cheam. Pleas by his parents to leave him alone and give him a chance were only moderately successful.

Partly because of this, partly because of his own shyness and inhibitions, Charles was never really happy at Cheam. Nor, at first, was he any happier at Gordonstoun and on one occasion he begged his grandmother to intercede with his parents to let him leave. But they made him stick it out and, looking back, he is glad they did.

His problems at school were not those of education. If never the most brilliant boy at either Cheam or Gordonstoun, neither was he the most backward. Painstaking and hard-working, his abilities lay somewhere in the middle. If he was poor at some subjects, like mathematics and physics, then he was good at others, English and French, history, geography and art.

His problems lay in the attitudes of those around him. His parents had hoped that in sending him to school he would be treated like "any other boy". It was a wish impossible of fulfilment. The teaching staff, with few exceptions, either genuflected to him or, going to the other extreme, came down on him hard to avoid accusations of favouritism. His schoolmates, similarly, either "crawled" to him—his own word—or bullied him or avoided him altogether.

At Cheam he had his head dunked in cold water. At Gordonstoun he was frequently the most knocked-about player on the rugby pitch. And there was always the Press watching him with hawk-like eyes, an enterprising freelance auctioning a book of princely essays, a female reporter quick to inform the world that he had had a sip of cherry brandy in a Stornoway pub. Both episodes upset him considerably and the memory of them rankled for years afterwards.

Hand in hand with schooldays went training for future monarchy. He was only thirteen when he attended his first palace luncheon. At sixteen he sat in on a meeting of the Duchy of Cornwall. At eighteen, like his mother before him, he was appointed a Counsellor of State.

It was not until he transferred from Gordonstoun to Timbertop in Australia at the age of seventeen that Charles began to enjoy his schooldays for the first time. In many respects, Timbertop, with its emphasis on the unorthodox and the great outdoors, was not all that dissimilar to Gordonstoun. But in one respect it differed radically. Boys and masters alike, with their more down-to-earth Australian attitude to royalty, neither crawled to him nor shied away. And judging by the fact that he was called " a pommy bastard " on more than one occasion, they certainly did not genuflect.

" More than any other experience, those years (in Australia) opened my eyes," Charles himself has said.

Back at Gordonstoun, he passed his ' A ' levels in history and French, and reportedly " shone " in the optional history paper. Nevertheless, the announcement that he was going to Trinity College, Cambridge, where his grandfather, the late King George VI, had been before him, was greeted with accusations that he was a " royal borderliner ".

His grandfather, during his spell at Trinity, lived a more or less segregated life in a specially rented house some distance from the college. Charles, by contrast, had two rooms on a " stair " shared by some ten other students. He tried eating in Hall, but was still shy enough to find this an ordeal and eventually had many of his meals in his rooms.

But gradually he began to mix more. From time to time he invited fellow students, among them a Welsh youngster who had worked on the buses before going to university, to his rooms for tea, biscuits and informal debate. He went to a few student parties, though seldom looking completely at ease; played cello with the college orchestra; went on a " dig " with a group of archaeological students and judged a beauty contest. If student contemporaries can be believed, he even took part in one or two " rags ", including one which resulted in the statue of Henry VIII which fronts the college being given a " third leg " made of papier mache. He went out with one or two girls, breaking the rules on one occasion by overstaying the permitted time-limit when visiting a girl-friend at Newnham College.

" I've never been as happy as I am at Cambridge," he confided in a friend around this time.

He joined an amateur acting group and took part in two revues in which he appeared in a number of different roles. Among other things, he was a weather forecaster announcing that " By morning promiscuity will be widespread ", a cello-playing rock star described as " The best plucker in the business " and a Victorian lecher boasting that " I like giving myself heirs ". For a royal prince it was all very daring.

All this, of course, was incidental to his main purpose. He attended lectures conscientiously, read voraciously and was often to be found working at the antique desk his mother had given him up to and beyond midnight. He graduated finally with an average B.A. (Hons) degree.

Inevitably, monarchical training and royal duties cut into his studies from time to time. He sat beside his mother for the state opening of Parliament and flew out to represent her at the memorial service to the late Harold Holt, Prime Minister of Australia. During one summer vacation he embarked upon a crash course designed by his father as an object-lesson in what lay ahead. He toured a newspaper plant in Edinburgh and government offices in Wales, went down a mine in Nottinghamshire, visited the docks at Tilbury and dived below the streets of London to chat with the human moles tunnelling a new subway. Back at college, he sandwiched flying lessons into an already crowded schedule and at the age of twenty, after fourteen and a half hours' tuition, heard his instructor say, " You're on your own, mate " and flew solo for the first time.

He was still a few months short of his twenty-first birthday when he was invested as Prince of Wales in the summer of 1969. Contrary to what some people think, Charles was not born Prince of Wales. The title is given or withheld at the discretion of the Sovereign and was bestowed on Charles by his mother when he was a schoolboy at Cheam. Neither is the ceremony the time-honoured one some people would have us believe. In fact, there had been only one previous investiture (at the instigation of the wily Lloyd George) and the Queen, initially, was not over-enthusiastic at the idea of repeating the performance. More in tune with public mood than you might think, she queried whether the timing was right—Welsh nationalists were on the rampage at the time—and thought it involved spending too much public money. Philip, too, queried " to what extent this sort of virtually medieval revival is necessary " and Charles himself said at one point that he would be glad when it was all over because it had become " a friction point for too many people."

The Queen's doubts were to prove well founded. A meeting in Cardiff's Temple of Peace to discuss the preliminaries was marked by an explosion which caused damage to the tune of several thousand pounds. Between then and the actual ceremony, seven and a half months later, there were to be twelve more bombings, the last being at Abergele in Denbighshire where two bombers blew themselves up with their own bomb.

Despite all this, the Investiture proved to be the most successful slice of royal ceremony since the Coronation even if security men nearly outnumbered the invited guests, helicopters patrolled overhead and minesweepers guarded the royal yacht. When she was crowned the Queen had felt that Charles, at four, was far too young to take the oath of allegiance. But now he did so. Colour television beamed the ceremony into six million homes in Britain and perhaps twenty-five times that number around the world, revealing the Queen as both monarch and mother. Mothers love straightening their sons' ties, but Charles's military uniform had no tie. So she adjusted the gold clasps of his ermine-trimmed robe instead.

The subsequent four-day tour Charles made of Wales was an equal success. In Cardiff alone over 70,000 people turned out to cheer him and the only demonstrator in sight had his protest banner forcibly wrenched from his grasp. By the time it was all over, Charles, not yet having acquired his mother's knack for multiple hand-shaking, had to have treatment to his right arm and shoulder.

Prince Philip, when he was younger, toyed with the idea of joining the Air Force, but was finally persuaded to enter the Navy instead. But Charles, since leaving university, has enjoyed the best of both worlds. First came a crash course at Cranwell R.A.F. College where he was given the rank of flight lieutenant, not as a sop to his royal status but as an acknowledgement of the flying experience he had already had. As at university, he quickly proved himself no royal goody-goody. He had been at Cranwell only three weeks when April Fool's Day came round . . . and an announcement over the public address system instructed fellow officers to hand in their shoes at the porter's lodge so that a heel design fault could be corrected. Many did. The idea, if not the actual announcement, came from the Prince of Wales.

Having absorbed from his father the philosophy that all life must include calculated risks, Charles insisted on being treated like any other trainee at Cranwell, even to the extent of completing his training with a parachute jump. Neither his mother nor the Government objected—a striking contrast to those not-so-long-ago days when a previous Prince of Wales who later became the Duke of Windsor was forced to give up steeplechasing because it was considered too risky.

His aircraft was flying at 1200 feet when Charles, in jump suit and crash helmet, baled out over the Channel. His feet tangled briefly in the rigging lines of his parachute. " Fortunately they weren't twisted round the lines and came out very quickly," he recalls.

Attending the passing-out parade at which Charles received his R.A.F. wings, his father was so delighted that, temporarily at least, he forgot his long-standing feud with the press photographers. Asked to shake hands with his son for their benefit, he quipped, " I'll stand on my head if you want me to."

Charles's passing-out report rated him an " above average " flyer and added that he would make " an excellent fighter pilot." But fighters were not what lay ahead. It was time now to switch from the R.A.F. to the Navy and Charles went to Dartmouth for a concentrated course in seamanship, navigation and marine engineering. This time it was Philip's uncle, Mountbatten of Burma, who attended his passing-out parade and who proudly revealed that " my nephew," as he referred to Charles, had come top of his class in navigation and seamanship.

Charles travelled to Gibraltar to join the guided missile destroyer *Norfolk* with the rank of sub-lieutenant. When the *Norfolk* returned later to Portsmouth, the Queen went along to see over her son's ship. Charles showed her round with a strip of plaster stuck on his chin to conceal a gash left by a flying polo ball.

Sea-going experience in the *Norfolk* was followed by further shore-based courses at Portsmouth and further flying experience, this time with naval aircraft, before Charles joined the frigate *Minerva* and subsequently the frigate *Jupiter*, at Singapore, as a watch-keeping officer. But naval duties frequently had to go hand-in-hand with royal chores, as when he opened the newly-

restored Prince of Wales Bastion on St Kitts, represented his
mother at Independence Day celebrations in the Bahamas, visited
Nepal for the coronation of King Birendra and toured Canada's
icebound Northwest Territories.

It was during his trip to Canada in 1975 that Charles dived
thirty feet under the ice at Resolute Bay, a point some 600 miles
inside the Arctic Circle. It was "bloody cold", he volunteered
when he surfaced again, then turned the whole thing into a right
royal joke by inflating his insulated diving suit to balloon-like
proportions. And it speaks volumes for the way he handles himself
that newspapermen who accompanied him on the trip, no
mean judges of character, voted it one of the best royal tours
ever.

There were occasional visits home where, pending the setting
up of his own establishment at Chevening, he had a three-room
bachelor pad at the front of the palace furnished with leather
armchairs, stereo equipment, his collection of soapstone carvings,
and shelves crammed with books on history, archaeology, art,
music and polo.

But long weeks at sea meant that he was out of the public eye
more than he had ever been since birth. He was doubtless grateful
for the fact. His spells at sea, as he revealed on television in
Australia, also left him little time for dating.

It was a television interview which underlined the big change
that has taken place in royal attitudes in recent years. The Queen
has never—could never—talk about herself in the way her son
talks about himself. Even Philip, though fairly revealing at times,
has never gone so far. Charles, however, seemed to have lost all
his earlier shyness and inhibitions as he talked freely about his
relationships with the opposite sex. He always warned any girl
who went out with him, he said, of what the consequences might
be.

"It's worse for her than it is for me," he said. "I have layers
of things to protect me." And he added this: "It does affect the
relationship and it can attract the wrong type of girl."

Ever since he was a small boy newspapers and magazines have
consistently tried to marry him off to this girl or that. He was
only four when one magazine first published a list of European
princesses he might one day marry. Needless to say, most of them
by now are married to someone else.

Charles himself had something to say about all this in a speech he made to the Parliamentary Press Gallery in 1975. He recalled the *brouhaha* which erupted over his reported romance with Lady Jane Wellesley, daughter of the Duke of Wellington, and the New Year she spent with him and his family at Sandringham.

" A crowd of 10,000 appeared when we went to church," he remembered. " Such was the obvious conviction that what they had read was true that I almost felt that I had better espouse myself at once so as not to disappoint so many people."

By this time he was learning to fly helicopters at Yeovilton prior to taking up duty with the Royal Marine Commandos aboard H.M.S. *Hermes*. And helicopter flying was not the only thing which came his way in Somerset. He also sampled scrumpy (strong cider) and went to see the X-certificate film *Percy's Progress*. By contrast, on leave in London, he went to the Royal Opera House to hear Verdi's *La Traviata*. He was in London at the time of the Moorgate Tube disaster and, a day or so later, went along to St Bartholomew's Hospital to visit Margaret Liles, the young policewoman whose foot had to be amputated before she could be freed from the wreckage. Nor was this any mere royal publicity exercise. In fact, Charles would have preferred it had the story of his visit not been made public and to this end did not even inform the local police that he was going to the hospital.

Charles has changed a great deal over the years. All youngsters change of course as they grow from boyhood to manhood, but in Charles the change seems to have been greater than most. The shy, blushing, foot-shuffling schoolboy of Cheam has matured into a young man of considerable character. In him can be seen his mother's strong sense of duty, his father's bluntness, the Queen Mother's humanity and, on rare occasions, his dead grandfather's famous temper.

That he possesses his grandfather's temper was demonstrated the day in Nassau when he leapt from his polo pony, stormed up three flights of steps, and told commentator Tom Oxley that his tongue-in-cheek remarks were turning the polo game into a barn dance.

If he lacks his father's sometimes caustic wit, he has something much more important : a real sense of humour, as he has revealed time and again. On the day of his parents' silver wedding anniversary, for instance, during a walkabout at the Barbican, he popped into a shop to say hello to the staff. Above him he spotted a sign : Drug Store.

" That's all I need," he said, grinning. " Someone to photograph me under that."

He was equally worried—or so he said—about the danger of being photographed in a compromising situation the day he met actress Susan Hampshire backstage at Windsor's Theatre Royal. Miss Hampshire was wearing the sort of dress which leaves little to the imagination. Said Charles, " My father told me if ever I met a lady in a dress like yours I must look her straight in the eyes. Otherwise someone might take a photograph of me in what might appear to be a compromising attitude."

He has a joke for most occasions. He once countered—or was perhaps agreeing with—an accusation that he was a " shabby dresser " by turning up at a full-dress evening function in an old tweed jacket. Another time, he launched into a speech—like his father, he writes his own—with the time-honoured joke about the bishop and the actress. He made a wisecrack about his appearance—he was swaddled in caribou fur at the time—during his visit to Canada's Northwest Territories, " I hope we don't meet a polar bear. He might think I'm in season."

It was during the same trip that he penned and sang a little ditty which went something like this :

> Impossible, unapproachable, God only knows,*
> The light's always dreadful and he won't damn well pose,
> Most maddening, most curious, he simply can't fail,
> It's always the same with the old Prince of Wales.
>
> Insistent, persistent, the Press never end,
> One day they will drive me right round the bend,
> Recording, rephrasing, every word that I say,
> It's got to be news at the end of the day.

Yet he is more than merely a royal comedian or an amusing after-dinner speaker. Like his father, he would seem to have the ability to see through to the core of a problem, as he revealed in a House of Lords debate in 1975. He had also, it would seem, benefited from his father's experience.

---

* Sung, we understand, to the tune: *Immortal, Invisible God Only Wise.*

Philip, years ago, was publicly castigated for extolling the virtues of national service. Charles carefully avoided the same trap by saying that there was no reasonable or logical justification for re-introducing national service. But, he went on, we ought to think of recreating some of the challenges of war in a peacetime situation so that adolescents could discover themselves and their capabilities through the challenge of adventure and hardship.

" It seems to me," said this young man, who has certainly had his own share of adventure, " that the problems we suffer in society through violence and anti-social behaviour on the part of some people are partly due to lack of outlets in which their energy, frustration and desire for adventure can be properly channelled."

A few weeks later he himself was diving through fifty feet of water off Portsmouth to explore the wreck of the *Mary Tudor*, once the pride of Henry VIII's navy.

9

The Queen's Homes

Prince Philip, who is seldom at a loss for a pithy phrase or witty expression, once referred to Buckingham Palace as " a tied cottage ". Previous residents have sometimes called it by harsher names. To Edward VII it was a " sepulchre " and to the Queen's father an " icebox ".

Edward VII, when he took over from Queen Victoria, quickly converted it from a " sepulchre " to something more lively and the more recent installation of central heating has ensured that it is no longer an " icebox ". But, in a sense, Philip is right about it being " a tied cottage ". It belongs to the nation—not the Queen —and goes with the job. But it is, of course, a tied cottage on a gigantic scale, so vast that to this day there are parts of it the Queen has never seen.

Her grandmother, Queen Mary, when she first went to live there, once found herself completely lost after taking a wrong turning. A former Mistress of the Robes was so nervous that the same fate might befall her that, during the twelve years she held office, she always insisted on being escorted to her apartment each time she went to the palace. Despite the advice, " The palace is built in a square; follow your nose and you can't go wrong," temporary staff, hired to augment the regulars on such occasions as a state banquet, sometimes do go wrong, ending up not only in the wrong room but even on the wrong floor.

Viewed from Prince Philip's helicopter as he choppers busily back and forth, the palace does indeed look like a hollow square. But seen from the inside it becomes a confusing labyrinth of elevators and stairways, red-carpeted corridors—some up to twenty feet wide and 200 feet long—and huge, high-ceilinged rooms. The number of rooms is usually given as " about 600 ".

But this, like the topography of the palace itself, is misleading. It depends on what you term " a room ". Deduct closets—some of them as big as a council house bedroom—loos and enclosed passages and the number of actual *rooms* shrinks rapidly to nearer the 300 mark.

Philip, with time on his hands when he and the Queen first moved in, set about exploring the whole place, from the (in those days) small cubicles, nicknamed " horse boxes ", in which the footmen slept on the top floor to the coal stores in the basement. In the course of doing so, he barged in on two startled housemaids enjoying their elevenses in one of the staff rooms. " Don't get up," he said, affably. " My mistake. I thought this was the post office."

The palace not only has its own post office (postal orders franked " Buckingham Palace " have been known to turn up in the pools) but also its own telephone exchange, police station and fire brigade. The Queen, when she first went to the palace as a small girl, was surprised and delighted to find postmen strolling the corridors to deliver the mail just as they do in any town or village.

Rooms and corridors alike are hung with old masters, furnished with antiques, stuffed with gifts given to generations of Royals. The methodically minded Queen Mary once set out to list all the gifts. Six years and 41,000 items later she accepted it as one of her few defeats in life.

In many ways, the palace is a self-contained little community, an island in the very heart of London, cut off from the rest of Britain by its own somewhat rarefied atmosphere. That, at least, is how newcomers to the staff usually feel at first.

It has its own sick bay and resident nurse. There is a sort of village shop—known as " the canteen "—where the staff can buy tea and biscuits, coffee and sweets, canned goods and beer. Dotted throughout the palace are 250 telephones, 300 clocks and so many windows that cleaning them, like painting the Forth Bridge, is an almost never-ending task. In the basement are fuel stores and rest rooms, storerooms and packing rooms, linen rooms, wine cellars and workshops. To the rear are the Royal Mews, with their own filling station and blacksmith's forge, an area where the ages of the horse and motor-car meet and overlap. The forty-acre garden, with its azaleas, lilac and laburnums, is a miniature wild-life sanctuary populated not only by the flamingoes the Queen was given some years ago, but by wild duck, geese, pigeons and a variety of butterflies.

A pigeon once made its nest on a window ledge of one of the state rooms. When eggs appeared in the nest someone told the Queen. She went along to see for herself and promptly gave instructions for the curtains to be drawn and the nest left undisturbed until the eggs had hatched out.

Originally the property of the Duke of Buckingham, the palace was known in Georgian times as Buckingham House. George III bought it from Buckingham for £21,000. But it was George IV who set about the mammoth and expensive task of turning it from a house into a palace. Parliament granted him what it thought was sufficient money, but by the time he died he had already spent three times the amount and the job was still incomplete.

When it was finally finished William IV liked the place so little that he never lived there. On his death, the eighteen-year-old Victoria moved in with delight. " At last I have a house of my own," she noted in her journal. However, she was later to complain that it was too small for her growing family and in " a dreadful state ".

More money was spent constructing a new front and, in the process, the original Marble Arch was moved to its present location. Edward VII installed electricity in place of gas and added more bathrooms, but by the time George V took over the stonework of the new front was already crumbling. Like William IV, he did not like the place and muttered that he would pull it down and go to live at Kensington Palace instead. But he stayed on and the crumbling front was refaced with Portland stone. Inside, according to the Duke of Windsor, there was " a dank, musty smell ".

Roughly speaking, the palace today can be divided into four main sections. There are the state apartments; the Queen's private apartment; the business offices occupied by the Queen's Private Secretary and Assistant Private Secretaries, by the Queen's Treasurer and Press Secretary, by clerks, typists and messengers; and the working and living quarters of those who run the palace as distinct from the monarchy. The Housekeeper and the Palace Steward each have their own apartment. So does the Queen's Dresser. Her apartment is immediately above the Queen's own private rooms and adjoins the rooms in which the extensive royal wardrobe is stored. Royal chefs live in an annexe adjoining the kitchens. Chauffeurs and grooms occupy flats above the stables and garages in the mews. Maids and footmen have rooms on the topmost floor, maids at the front and men at the back of the palace.

Until quite recent times royal footmen still lived much as they did in the days of Dickens, sleeping in a single long dormitory divided into cubicles. The Queen's father never liked the arrangement and wanted to change it, but first one thing, then another—the war and the economic conditions which followed the war—prevented him from getting round to it. The Queen has finally done what her father could not and the old-fashioned " horse boxes " have now been replaced by comfortable bed-sitters, each with its own wash-basin, wardrobe, chest-of-drawers, writing table and easy chair.

The state apartments, which come to life only for investitures, banquets and suchlike occasions, occupy about one third of the total floor space of the palace. They represent one of the most magnificent unexploited tourist attractions in London, though the day may well come—indeed, may have come by the time this book is published—when they will be open to the public as the state apartments at Windsor already are. Tourists would surely queue six deep and a mile long for an opportunity to see the Throne Room with its friezes depicting the Wars of the Roses, the brilliant shimmer of the State Dining-Room, the Bow Room with its Corinthian columns, the 1844 Room (so named after a visit in that year by the Tsar of Russia), the 1855 Room (similarly named after a visit by Napoleon III), the Blue, White and Green Drawing-Rooms, and the Royal Closet. It is in the Royal Closet that the Queen and her entourage muster on state occasions. When all is ready the touch of a concealed spring causes one of the china cabinets in the adjoining room to swing back for the royal party to make a surprise and effective entrance.

Most magnificent of all the state rooms is the ballroom, a vast arena some 123 feet long, 65 feet wide and 45 feet high, illuminated by six glittering chandeliers, its walls hung with tapestries depicting Jason's search for the Golden Fleece. It is in the ballroom that investitures are held, with the Queen hanging

The Queen in casual, weekend
clothes

The Queen and Prince Philip pay
silent tribute to the lost children
of Aberfan, 1966

A Derby to remember. The Queen and the Queen Mother watch
Lester Piggott about to win the 1968 race

The Queen in a gay mood, chatting to Princess Anne during a
break in the Maori display at Suva, Fiji, 1970

medals on special hooks attached to the jackets of those being decorated. It is here too that state banquets are held when visiting monarchs or presidents come to call.

For weeks ahead of a state banquet the quaintly-named Yeoman of the Gold and his assistants are kept busy polishing what is known as " the royal gold ", though much of it is actually silver gilt. The extent of the job can be gauged from the fact that the whole lot is said to weigh around five tons and one table centre at least is so massive that it takes four men to lift it and set it in place. The collection is carefully checked after each banquet to ensure that nothing is missing. Very occasionally something is. A gold plate was returned once by an embarrassed footman who had taken some left-over ice cream to his room for a late-night snack.

As the big day approaches, housemaids dust and polish the ballroom furniture. Damask tablecloths dating from Victoria's day are brought up from the linen room on trolleys. Each place setting is checked with a measuring stick to ensure that goblets and cutlery are as precisely arrayed as a Guards regiment on parade.

The day of the banquet finds the palace almost bulging at the seams with extra staff, perhaps as many as 150 temporaries hired through an employment agency. Pages and footmen don their state liveries, kept between times in mothproof containers. Pages wear black and gold tunics with black knee-breeches. Footmen have scarlet tunics and breeches of scarlet and gold. But neither pages nor footmen any longer " powder " their hair, a messy business which involved coating their heads with a nauseous mixture of soap and water, flour and starch. Prince Philip put a stop to that, regarding it as " unmanly ".

Flowers and plants, roses, lilies and orchids entwined with grapes are banked in the corners of the ballroom. There are more flowers in the vases on the tables. But those in front of the Queen float in a low bowl so that she can be clearly seen by her guests. When all is ready, word is sent to the Queen so that she can inspect things for herself.

The Queen was heard to say once, with obvious satisfaction, that a state banquet at Buckingham Palace always " runs like clockwork ". The same is not true of all the countries she has visited during her years of monarchy. There was one banquet

K

overseas where she found herself already eating her sweet while guests at the far end of the room were still waiting for their soup. That this sort of thing never happens at Buckingham Palace represents a considerable feat of organization when you consider that the food has to be humped through quarter-of-a-mile of corridors and stairways to get it from the kitchens to the ballroom. The timing is helped by a system of miniature "traffic lights" which direct servants when to serve and when to clear away dirty plates.

The Queen's entrance into the ballroom on the occasion of a state banquet is regal in the extreme, with guests standing smartly to attention, a band playing the National Anthem and two courtiers backing away in front of her with lowered gaze. Her departure on one occasion at least was strikingly different. Hardly was she out of the ballroom than she removed both shoes and tiara before heading for her own room. En route she encountered a member of her personal staff. Unabashed, she clapped a hand to the small of her back and feigned a hobble. " Ow, me poor aching back," she moaned in mock Cockney.

Comparatively few people get to see the inside of Buckingham Palace. Tourists can visit the Royal Mews on certain days or inspect a selection of royal pictures in the Queen's Gallery. Those with sufficient nerve can briefly penetrate the Privy Purse door at the front of the palace to sign the visitors' book. But only if the Queen is in residence. Banquet guests and those being decorated get to see the ballroom, though most who go there for the first time remember it afterwards as only a vague blur. Burly Ron Russell, who went there to receive his George Medal after saving Anne from a would-be kidnapper, recalls being " almost overpowered " by it all . . . " so many rooms, such long corridors, so many paintings and antiques."

Luncheon guests penetrate to the Bow Room, where the young Victoria was betrothed to her beloved Albert, and the adjoining 1844 Room. Garden party guests also get to see the Bow Room on their way through. They may even be briefly detained there if the National Anthem is already being played in the garden beyond.

But only royal relatives and a few close friends ever get to see the Queen's private apartment.

" We live above the shop," Prince Philip said once, and this, in a sense, is true. The royal apartment is on the first floor, its windows looking out towards Constitution Hill.

Focal point of the apartment is the large bay-windowed sitting-room which also doubles as the Queen's study. It is a comfortably cluttered room, usually fragrant with the scent of carnations, the Queen's favourite flowers, in which the homeliness of family photos, piled-up magazines and snoozing corgis contrasts vividly with the leather-covered dispatch box standing on a side table beside the Queen's desk. There may be a saucer of dog biscuits on another side table and there is always a bowl of drinking water on the floor near the door. A settee and matching armchairs flank the marble fireplace. The Queen's desk stands in the bay-window recess and a glass-fronted cabinet holds the collection of jade inherited from Queen Mary. A chandelier of Waterford glass lights the room at night and in winter logs burn in the fireplace to reinforce the central heating.

Philip's study, further along the corridor, is more businesslike, filled with gadgets and remote control buttons. It was not always like that. In the days when it was the Queen's father's study it was as elegantly old-fashioned as the rest of the palace rooms.

The Queen's sitting-room is flanked on one side by the private dining-room and on the other by her bedroom with its double bed. Off the bedroom is her dressing-room and bathroom. Philip has his own bathroom and dressing-room next door.

The dining-room, with its oval-shaped mahogany table and three matching sideboards, looks at its best when the Queen is expecting friends to dinner and the table is set with Georgian cutlery around a silver statuette of the Queen on horseback flanked by four protective guardsmen. Unless they are entertaining, no servants wait on the Queen and her husband at dinner. Instead they help themselves from silver dishes kept warm on hotplates.

Around the corner at the far end of the apartment is the Audience Room in which the Queen receives the Prime Minister and others. Opposite is the room in which the royal corgis sleep and another room in which dressmakers and others wait until the Queen is ready for them. Nearby is a room still known as the Tea Room, though it is a long time since it last witnessed the quaint old English ceremony of afternoon tea. These days it might more appropriately be known as the Gift Room. With so many relatives and friends, the Queen has constantly to find suitable gifts for Christmas, birthdays, anniversaries, weddings and christenings. To avoid being caught napping, she maintains a small reserve stock of gifts suitable for different occasions in the the old Tea Room.

But Buckingham Palace is only one of the Queen's four main residences (five if you include the sombre Palace of Holyrood-house in Edinburgh where she stays for about one week in the year). Windsor Castle, like Buckingham Palace, belongs to the nation. Sandringham and Balmoral, by contrast, are her private property.

If Buckingham Palace is large, Windsor Castle is vast, with walls so thick that the Queen's father, requiring an extra bathroom, found space for it in the thickness of a wall. For more than nine centuries it has been the stronghold of successive British monarchs. It was William the Conqueror who first fortified the mound on which the castle stands. The present keep (known as the Round Tower) was built by Henry II. Edward III turned it from a castle into a palace and George IV tried to turn the clock back by adding towers and battlements which were no longer necessary.

By comparison with some of her ancestors, the Queen's alterations have been modest in the extreme. With Philip's help, she has turned the old Orangery into a swimming pool, re-designed part of the garden (Philip actually did the designing by sticking bits of foam rubber, representing roses, on a wooden base) and remodelled the old Victoria Tower, now known as the Queen's Tower, so that it affords a home within a castle. She now has a light airy study in which to work when at Windsor and the old Oak Dining-Room has been transformed into a bright and cheerful drawing-room with deep sofas, comfortable arm-chairs and a pair of antique Chinese cabinets which are not quite what they seem. One conceals a record player while the other holds drinks. There are pictures by contemporary artists on the walls and a statuette of the Queen's famous racehorse, Aureole, has a place of honour.

Horses and racing are the Queen's twin passions, as they were for Queen Anne. It was the portly Anne, tired of journeying all the way to Newmarket for the races, who decided to have her own racecourse on the doorstep. That was 250 years ago and it cost her £1,000. The result was Royal Ascot.

For the Queen, Royal Ascot is one of the social high spots of the year. She moves over from Buckingham Palace to Windsor for the week and invites relatives and racegoing friends to join her. But as always with her, work comes first. First thing after breakfast each morning she deals with the contents of her boxes. Only then does she go out riding with her guests. After lunch the Queen, along with her relatives and guests, sets off for Duke's Lane where a cavalcade of open carriages awaits them. The Queen and Prince Philip, along with the Master of the Queen's Horse, ride in the first carriage. Royal relatives and friends take it in turns to fill the other six. Then it is off to the races in style, with outriders, postillions and footmen in their scarlet and gold liveries lending colour to the scene.

In the evening comes dinner in the State Dining-Room. Before dinner a page trots round swinging a pot of smouldering lavender, essential a century or more ago to combat the smell of the castle drains. Windsor's drains no longer smell, but the custom continues. The dining table is set with gold plate and antique china shipped over from Buckingham Palace. A portrait of Queen Victoria, who once cautioned her son Bertie against going to Ascot too often, looks down disapprovingly. Background music, from Strauss waltzes to the latest pop tunes, is provided by musicians from the Brigade of Guards.

As many as forty people sit down to dinner each night, waited on by pages and footmen wearing what are known as " semi-state " liveries. After dinner there may be a film show in the Throne Room, converted into a cinema by the installation of a screen and duel sound projectors, or the carpet may be rolled back for dancing in the Crimson Drawing-Room.

If Windsor is a real castle, steeped in history and tradition, Balmoral Castle is not. It dates back only to the mid-nineteenth century when the estate was bought from Sir Robert Gordon for £31,500. Albert bought it sight unseen for Victoria, thought the house far too small when he did finally get round to seeing it, pulled it down and built the present quaint cross between a German *schloss* and the stronghold of a Highland chief.

The Queen loves Balmoral, as her great-great-grandmother, Queen Victoria, did before her. To Victoria, it was always " our home in the Highlands ". Her great-great-grand-daughter has called it " My favourite spot."

Much of Balmoral is still much as it was in Victoria's day . . . mounted stags' heads in the corridors, portraits of Victoria, Albert and their many children in the dining-room, paintings by Landseer, mounted rams' heads (which once served as snuff-boxes) on the sideboards, lampholders carved in the form of Highland shepherds. Some of the heavily embossed wallpaper still bears Victoria's VRI cypher and in the marble-floored entrance hall the tattered banners of Highland regiments hang above a statue of the Prince Consort in full Highland regalia.

Successive generations of royal children have not always had the same veneration for Albert as Queen Victoria did and the statue has been the butt of various japes over the years. There was one occasion when Albert's intellectual features were given a quite different appearance by the application of lipstick and face powder, and another when an important visitor, having deposited his hat and coat on a chair before seeing the Queen, emerged from her room again to find that the Prince Consort was now wearing them.

The heathery acres of Balmoral afford the Queen and her family a combination of privacy and freedom such as they cannot always find elsewhere. At Balmoral there is seldom need for the Queen to " dress up and queen it ". Instead, she can relax in the sort of casual, comfortable clothes she prefers, often a tartan skirt worn with a tweed jacket. Philip wears a kilt much of the time. Andrew and Edward alternate between kilts and jeans. At Balmoral the Queen can ride without restraint—but only after the contents of the boxes have been tackled. At Balmoral she can go for long, striding walks with the dogs, the corgis doing their best to keep pace with the labradors from Sandringham, the Queen calling them to heel if necessary with a piercing whistle at which she is curiously adept.

Balmoral is a place to continue the old traditions. Each morning the Queen's piper parades up and down outside. Each evening a trio of pipers parades round the dining table. A visit to the Highland Games is a regular feature of the summer vacation. The Gillies' Ball is another.

Highland dancing was part and parcel of the Queen's up-bringing. It was not part of Philip's young life and when the pair of them visited Edinburgh soon after their wedding he found himself standing idly by while someone else partnered his wife in a double eightsome reel. Philip is not a man to let that sort of thing happen more than once. He took a crash course in Highland dancing and two nights later, at another ball, partnered his wife himself. These days, at the Gillies' Ball, clad in full Highland dress, he heads the opening Grand March with the Queen before separating from her to join sets made up of gillies and their wives, servants and soldiers from the guard-of-honour.

In some ways, Sandringham, on Norfolk's windswept coast, is not unlike Balmoral. It has the same sense of freedom and privacy, and the surrounding district, with its pines and heathland, is like a Scottish landscape in miniature.

Like Balmoral, it affords the Queen freedom to walk in private, to ride at leisure, to drive herself about the quiet roads which honeycomb the area. She was out driving one winter when her car became trapped in a snowdrift. She abandoned the car and trudged through the snow to the nearest house, from where she telephoned Sandringham with a view to obtaining assistance. But the duty telephone operator, though well accustomed to handling outgoing calls for the Queen, had never received an incoming call which started with the words, " This is the Queen speaking." He thought someone was playing a joke on him and his initial reaction was such as to require embarrassed apologies when it finally dawned on him that it really was the Queen on the line.

The Sandringham estate cost £220,000 when it was first bought by the Queen's great-grandfather, the Prince of Wales who later became Edward VII. More accurately, it was bought *for him* by his parents, Victoria and Albert, who hoped it would get him away from the temptations of London. But Bertie, as he was known to relatives and friends, subsequently took his own temptations, including the delectable Lillie Langtry, to Sandringham with him.

As at Balmoral, the house of today is not the original one. That proved to be so damp that Bertie tore it down and built afresh. The dampness persisted, however, and even in the Queen's childhood was so bad that water ran down the walls of the servants' quarters in wet weather.

Like her great-grandfather before her, the Queen, a year or so back, had ambitious plans for renovating and re-building Sandringham. The job was put in hand and the Queen herself took over a farmhouse at nearby Wolferton in order to have somewhere to stay in the area while work on the " Big House " was in progress. The first stage of the work involved the demolition of ninety-one of Sandringham's 361 rooms and this had been largely completed when things came to an abrupt halt. Inflation had sent costs soaring and, whether or not she could still afford it, the Queen felt it wrong to be spending so much of her private money at a time when she was asking Parliament for an increased Civil List to meet the rising expenses of monarchy.* She ordered what had already been done at Sandringham to be made weathertight and announced her intention of joining the stately homes league by throwing its doors open to the public.

* Chapter 11.

10

All The Queen's Men

Buckingham Palace has many doors. There is the Grand Entrance from which the Queen departs in state for such top-level functions as the opening of Parliament and the Garden Entrance which she uses for more informal comings and goings. There is what is known as the King's Door which Prince Philip sometimes finds it more convenient to use. Early in the present reign it was suggested that it should be re-named the Queen's Door, but the Queen preferred to stick to the old name in memory of her father. There is the Trade Door in Buckingham Palace Road, where the meat and veg, eggs and milk are delivered daily. And there is the Privy Purse Door, at the front right-hand corner of the palace, which is used by those whose job it is to master-mind the various facets of the Queen's life. They are known as the Queen's Household.*

Like much else about the Monarchy, the structure of the Queen's Household is complex in the extreme, an intricate present-day mixture of ancient tradition and modern necessity. On paper, the latest list available at the time this book was being written runs to a staggering total of 384 names, ranging from the Lord Chamberlain through Gentlemen Ushers and Extra Gentle-men Ushers, through Gentlemen at Arms and Yeomen of the Guard, to the Royal Company of Archers who are headed by a belted earl with the quaintly anachronistic title of Captain General and Gold Stick for Scotland. In practice, however, perhaps rather more than 300 of the 384 names listed can be discounted as being the holders of traditional posts who are today required to perform only occasional ceremonial duties. Consider the Yeomen of the Guard, for instance, or the Gentlemen at

* Appendix V.

Arms. In the good old bad old days, the Yeomen had the tricky task of tasting the monarch's food as a precaution against possible food poisoning, while the Gentlemen at Arms actually defended the Palace of Westminster during the Wyatt rebellion of the sixteenth century. But food poisoning is no longer common in royal circles and the long-handled battle axes of the Gents at Arms would be of very little avail in the event of any present-day Wyatt trying to storm the Palace of Buckingham.

Remove such names from the list and you are left with a residue of perhaps sixty to eighty who work for the Queen on a salaried day-to-day basis, not including the royal ladies-in-waiting The Queen's ladies-in-waiting are not paid a salary, though they do get an honorarium to meet clothing and other expenses. But their work is more than merely ceremonial even if their titles still have the ring of history about them: Mistress of the Robes; Ladies and Women of the Bedchamber.

Working to a rota, they take it in turns to reside at the palace and attend upon the Queen. Theoretically they are on call from the time she gets up in the morning until she retires at night. In practice, they deal with what might be termed her "semi official" mail—answering letters seeking charity donations or merely wishing the Queen well—as well as accompanying her on her public engagements. When the Queen sallies forth it is the duty of the lady-in-waiting to ensure that she has everything she may conceivably require, umbrella and waterproof cape if it turns to rain, sunglasses if the sun is bright, spare white gloves in case those she is wearing become soiled, spare shoes in case she wrenches a heel, handkerchiefs, cosmetics and barley sugar (as an antidote to possible travel sickness).

The structure of the Queen's Household can perhaps best be likened to a pyramid with the Queen as its apex. Immediately below her come the five key men who overlord the various departments of her public and official life. They are the Lord Chamberlain, the Private Secretary, the Keeper of the Privy Purse, the Master of the Household and the Crown Equerry, each with his own staff of deputies, assistants, clerks and typists.

The most senior member of the Household is the Lord Chamberlain who does not, in fact, operate from Buckingham Palace but from St James's Palace nearby. Symbol of his authority is the gold key he wears at his hip when attending the Queen on state occasions. He has also another symbol of office, a white wand (or staff). On the death of a monarch, the Lord Chamberlain, as a last act of service, breaks the wand in two and casts the pieces into the funeral vault.

On a more practical level the Lord Chamberlain is responsible for arranging such things as investitures, garden parties, in fact all royal ceremonies with a few important exceptions, among them the coronation and the funeral of the monarch which remain the traditional responsibility of the Earl Marshal of England. It is the Lord Chamberlain who advises the Queen on who to invite to state functions, on the order of precedence on such occasions and on such things as correct and incorrect attire for a particular occasion.

A previous holder of the post once decreed that women in trouser suits could not be admitted to the royal enclosure at Ascot (though he apparently saw no harm in admitting dolly birds wearing the most miniature of mini-skirts). That the Queen herself had no particular aversion to trouser suits was surely apparent from the fact that she did not blink an eyelid, that same month, when Lady Chichester turned up in one to watch her sailor-husband knighted at Greenwich.

Guest lists, order of precedence and whether or not women should wear trouser suits are not, of course, the beginning and end of the Lord Chamberlain's functions. He also oversees the royal chapels, the royal library and art collection, and the royal swans. He appoints royal physicians, royal chaplains and the Poet Laureate. He issues royal warrants.

The issue of a royal warrant is not the signal for someone to be hauled off to the Tower of London on a charge of high treason. On the contrary, it is a badge of distinction awarded to those who supply goods or provide services to the Queen. Traders and manufacturers granted a royal warrant can display the royal arms outside their premises, on their vans and on their notepaper, in their advertising and on their products. But only on those products they actually supply to the Queen, and a manufacturer who supplies, say, pickles cannot also display the royal arms on his bottles of tomato ketchup. And any advertising must be discreet, dignified and the epitome of good taste. For the royal arms to appear alongside some such slogan as " The Queen Wears Our Panti-Hose " would never do.

Despite such limitations, royal warrants are both eagerly sought after and highly prized. " They are the best advertisement that money *can't* buy," one warrant-holder told us and the Royal Warrant Holders' Association has devoted not a little time and trouble over the years to tracking down and nailing those who would have the public believe that they supply the Queen when in fact they do not. In Britain such instances are rare. They are more frequent overseas, though even then the Association can frequently intervene successfully as it did when it stopped a distiller in Greece from retailing whisky with what appeared to be Britain's royal arms on the labels.

Aware of the considerable benefits which can follow from royal patronage, some traders go to quite extraordinary lengths. One exhibitor at an agricultural show in New Zealand even laid his own forty-yard stretch of red carpet at an angle to that laid down for the Queen's tour of the show. Surprisingly, the trick worked. The Queen and Philip shot off at a tangent and ended up inspecting a two-room holiday chalet not included in their official itinerary.

Over her years of monarchy, the Queen (through the Lord Chamberlain) has issued 655 warrants so far. They cover almost every conceivable royal requirement, from footmen's liveries to dog food, from bagpipes to nosegays, from champagne to sausages. Warrants have been issued to such world-famous names as Rolls-Royce and to small shopkeepers unknown outside their own locality, like R. F. and J. Scoles, the village butchers at Dersingham, Norfolk, who supply the Queen with her meat when she goes to Sandringham. Philip, in addition, has issued fifty-eight warrants. Up to the end of 1975, at least, the present Prince of Wales had not granted any warrants, though there are five still held by those who catered for the late Duke of Windsor in the days when he was Prince of Wales.

If the Lord Chamberlain is the most senior of the Queen's Household, he is not, these days, perhaps the most influential. That honour goes to the Private Secretary, a post currently held by Lieutenant-Colonel the Right Honourable Sir Martin Charteris, who has been described as looking " like a character out of Bulldog Drummond." He has been with the Queen, in one capacity or another, since she was a bride in her twenties. He was her Private Secretary in the days when she was a Princess and was with her in Kenya when news reached her of her father's death. But he lacked the experience to continue as her Private Secretary in those early days when she was first Queen. To advise her in those days, she fell back upon Sir Alan Lascelles, who had been Private Secretary to her father before her. Charteris became one of her Assistant Private Secretaries, first under Lascelles and later under Sir Michael (later Lord) Adeane, and it was not until Adeane's retirement in 1972 that he achieved his present important position.

As Private Secretary, he is the first member of the Household to see the Queen each morning. He ploughs through the contents of her boxes with her, plans her schedules, helps draft her speeches. He sees the Queen every day and sometimes more than once a day. He accompanies her on state visits and Commonwealth tours. When she weekends at Windsor, so—often—does he. When she goes to Balmoral, so does he. With rare exceptions, he is always within call and on call.

Previous Private Secretaries have been involved in affairs of state at the highest and most delicate levels. Had the Queen's uncle, during his brief reign as Edward VIII, heeded the advice of his Private Secretary, Sir Alexander Hardinge (that the divorced Mrs Simpson should leave the country without delay), there might not have been an Abdication.

Hardinge's successor, Sir Alan Lascelles, was more successful in dissuading the Queen's father from sailing with the D-Day invasion fleet. Churchill was going, so the King would go too—until Lascelles asked him what advice he would be expected to tender to the new Queen as to her choice of a prime minister in event that neither the King nor Churchill returned from their dangerous outing.

The King took his point. As a result, he not only changed his mind about being where the action was on D-Day, but exercised sufficient royal authority to prevail upon Churchill to do likewise.

To assist him in his role of Private Secretary Charteris commands the services of a Deputy Private Secretary, an Assistant Private Secretary, a Secretary to the Private Secretary, a Press Secretary and two Assistant Press Secretaries as well as miscellaneous clerks and typists. Of all these, it is perhaps the Press Secretary who occupies the traditionally hottest seat, though the temperature is lower now than it was in the early years of the Queen's reign. In those days, the advent of a young new Queen was interpreted in some quarters, rightly or wrongly, as a signal that the regal curtain between monarch and subjects could be finally ripped apart and torn down. The then Press Secretary, the late Commander Richard Colville, a courtier of the old school, did not see things in quite the same light. The Queen, he insisted, had a right to a private life and he intended to see that she got it. As a result, newspaper editors labelled him "unco-operative" and one went so far as to say in print that Colville was doing a good job in ensuring "that an absolute minimum is published about anything of interest concerning the Royal Family."

Colville's retirement in 1968 saw him succeeded by William Heseltine, an Australia, who set out to project a more modern image of the Queen. One result was the television film *Royal Family*. That his efforts pleased his royal employer is apparent from the fact that he now holds the post of Assistant Private Secretary. His successor as Press Secretary resigned after only eighteen months following what was described as "a difference of opinion" and the traditional "hot seat" has since been occupied by Ronald Allison, who is perhaps better known to the public at large for his previous sports commentaries than for his work as court correspondent.

Of the other three top men in the Royal Household, the Keeper of the Privy Purse watches over royal finances, the Crown Equerry runs the garages and stables in the royal mews and the Master of the Household, among other things, has charge of the palace fabric and furnishings. As Master of the Household, Sir Peter Ashmore is, in a sense, the Queen's major-domo. Of the palace staff of 337 full-time and 126 part-time employees, perhaps half come under his jurisdiction. To aid him in his mammoth task he has the help of three principal lieutenants, his Assistant, the Palace Steward and the Housekeeper.

Between them, calling upon the assistance of maids and cleaning women, electricians and plumbers, upholsterers and carpet-layers, carpenters and french polishers, they ensure that the palace is kept clean, that heating, lighting, plumbing and elevators are all in good working order, that windows are washed and clocks wound, that frayed carpets and worn curtains are repaired or replaced, that the valuable antique furniture is properly cared for. The Housekeeper has charge of the housemaids and cleaning women; also of the vast linen room in the basement with its piles of sheets and tablecloths, pillow cases and table napkins, towels and dusters. The housemaids usually work in teams of two, one finishing at lunchtime and the other remaining on duty until early evening. Next day they switch round. Under the Palace Steward come the pages and the footmen as well as the Yeomen of the Cellars, the Gold, the Silver and Glass. The four pages known as Pages of the Back Stairs attend personally upon the Queen and Prince Philip. They and their attendant footmen take it in turns to work through the day until the royal couple retire at night, then have the next day off. Other pages and footmen, like the housemaids, work to a rota which enables some of them to finish at lunchtime and others later.

The Master of the Household also serves as a buffer between the Queen and the harsher realities of the present-day employer-employee relationship. The Queen has never yet had a strike on her hands at Buckingham Palace, but there was one occasion, some years back, when royal servants threatened a sit-in. The trouble was not over wages but food and matters came to a head one evening with a complaint that there were too many cold meals being served.

" We want something hot and we're sitting here until we get it," said the man elected to act as spokesman.

The sit-in was soon ended, however, when egg and chips were dished up to supplement the cold meat and salad already available.

In a Britain where the term ' servant ' has become almost a dirty word, there have occasionally been other problems. Older members of the ' staff ' may still rate the honour and glory of working for the Queen as more important than wages and hours of work, but newcomers do not always see things in the same loyal light. Nor, perhaps, do they find quite the glitter and glamour they had expected from palace life. As a result, some stay only a short time before moving on.

Nor, in an era of rampant inflation and difficulty in making ends meet, has ' moonlighting ' been entirely unknown among royal servants. A palace chauffeur once took an additional part-time job as driver for a car-hire firm. Palace maids have been known to help out as cloakroom attendants at embassy functions in London and footmen have turned themselves into waiters for private parties.

And there was one occasion when the Upstairs and Downstairs of royal life met in rather surprising circumstances. The Queen was dining out privately. If the face of the ' waiter ' who served her during dinner seemed vaguely familiar it was hardly to be wondered at. It was one of her own staff from Buckingham Palace.

The Queen with President Nyerere of Tanzania, in the 1844
room at Buckingham Palace, 1975

A shower of confetti covers the Queen and Prince Philip on a
state visit to Mexico during the 1975 visit

Royalty toasts royalty. The Queen and Emperor Hirohito in
Japan, 1975

I I

The Cost

In recent years, nothing about Britain's monarchy has excited so much controversy as its cost. In particular, how much money the Queen should be allowed each year to meet her expenses. Note that we do not say " how much the Queen is paid each year ", for she no longer receives a salary from the state in the sense, say, that the prime minister does. On the other hand, the amount allowed her for expenses, substantial though it may seem, is only a fraction of the total cost of monarchy.

In the ensuing argument—which erupted in Parliament in 1971 and again in 1975 (when eighty-nine members of the House of Commons voted against a proposal to allow the Queen more money to cope with soaring inflation)—related financial matters have tended to be drawn into the discussion. How much the Queen is worth, for instance, and whether she should pay tax on her private income. Neither point has any real bearing on the overall argument.

Nevertheless, public curiosity about the size of the Queen's fortune is understandable. Guesses—and they can have been little more—have put the size of her personal fortune as low as £3 million and as high as £50-£100 million. The latter figure is so wild of the mark that it is said to have " upset " the Queen when she read it and even the former would seem to have been on the high side, certainly at the time it was originally estimated.

The figure of £50-£100 million, bandied around during the 1971 controversy over royal money, brought some fairly blunt speaking from Lord Cobbold, the then Lord Chamberlain. The royal palaces, the crown jewels and the royal collections were indeed of astronomical value, he told a Parliamentary Select Committee. But these, he added, were in no sense the Queen's

L

private property. They were merely invested in her as the Sovereign to be handed over, in due course, to her successor.

The Sandringham and Balmoral estates, he conceded, were indeed her private property, but suggestions being made in some quarters that, even apart from these, the Queen had a private fortune which might run as high as £50 million or more were " wildly exaggerated ".

So, how rich is the Queen?

In what would seem to have been an inspired interview, John Colville, her Private Secretary in the days when she was Princess Elizabeth, and subsequently a director of Coutts and Co., where she banks her money, offered to " eat my hat " if her personal fortune ran to more than £2 million. Despite this rather flamboyant offer, the size of the Queen's fortune was again being put at " up to £50 million " by at least one newspaper when the controversy erupted again in 1975 and the same figure will doubtless be cited afresh in the future.

The question remains : what has the Queen's private money to do with how much she should be granted each year to meet the expenses of monarchy? There would seem to be no more reason for these expenses to be geared to her private fortune than for those of a travelling salesman to depend on how much he has in the post office savings bank or those of a company to be based on how much the chairman was left by his parents. And no more reason why the Queen should disclose details of her private money simply to satisfy public and parliamentary curiosity than for a prime minister to reveal how much he was paid for his memoirs.

Whether the Queen should pay tax on her private income and whether Capital Transfer tax should be paid when her heir succeeds her are other matters entirely. These are perhaps legitimate topics for public debate, though such debate is usually based more on emotion than logic, differing attitudes seeming to depend on whether the speaker regards the monarch as being above the law or merely, to borrow a phrase, as a civil servant with a crown on his or her head.

For generations past (certainly back to the days of William and Mary) there has been controversy over the paying of Britain's monarchs. William was allowed £700,000 a year, a fortune in those seventeenth-century days. Out of it, he had to upkeep the royal palaces, pay the judges and such civil servants as there were. But Parliament, to make it quite clear who ran what, paid the army.

The Georges, however, found even £700,000 insufficient and the amount was upped by stages to £850,000. In return, George III agreed to surrender to Parliament what were then known as the Crown Lands (now the Crown Estates) with the exception of the Duchies of Lancaster and Cornwall.

How far the Crown may have had any legal right to these Lands (or Estates) in the first place is a fine debating point of which socialists have occasionally made good use. Be that as it may, the deal with George III has since proved an excellent bargain from the parliamentary viewpoint.

The Crown Estates run to several hundred thousand acres in England and Scotland with a few acres also in Wales. The acreage is mainly agricultural, but it is the smaller non-agricultural acreage which is by far the most valuable. Much of Regent Street, Piccadilly and the Haymarket in London—offices and shops, restaurants and theatres—stand on land forming part of the Crown Estates. There is also property in Carlton House Terrace and Victoria; Hackney and Tower Hamlets, Fulham and Southwark; further holdings in the City of London and at Windsor and Ascot.

At the time of their original surrender to Parliament the Crown Lands had an income of approximately £89,000 a year and a surplus, after deducting expenses, of about £11,000. So George III was on to a good thing. But times have changed. The last available figures (for 1973-4) reveal an income of £8,900,000—one hundred times that of 1760—and a surplus revenue, for the Exchequer, of £5,200,000.

So much for the public side of things. Now to look at the Queen's private money. The young Victoria had no money at all when she succeeded to the throne. But she soon learned about money matters from the economical Albert and his teachings were to be allied to a frugal way of life after his death. So much so that, out of a state allowance of £385,000 a year, on which she voluntarily paid income tax (the equivalent of threepence in the pound in those days before Parliament grabbed such a large chunk of the national income), she still managed to save.

Details of royal wills are not made public, so there is no way of knowing what Queen Victoria left when she died or to whom it was left. But there is reason to think that her son, Edward VII, inherited around £2 million from Mama when he took over the throne. Bertie, as he was known in the family circle, certainly did not live frugally. On the contrary, he was frequently in debt. However, he also had the benefit in his later years of shrewd advice from two of the most brilliant financiers of the day, Baron Maurice de Hirsch and Sir Ernest Cassell. As a result, his reign ended with about as much in the Royal Family's private kitty as when it started.

The bulk of what he left went to his only surviving son, George V, who, if he did not live as frugally as his grandmother had, was far from being as extravagant and high-living as his father. It was on his death that the royal fortune ran into trouble. As far as is known, the bulk of what George V left, including Balmoral (which Victoria had bought) and Sandringham (which Edward VII added to the family holdings), went to the eldest son who succeeded him as Edward VIII. The other three sons, the Dukes of York (the Queen's father), Kent and Gloucester, received smaller inheritances—probably less than £1 million apiece. With Edward VIII's abdication to become Duke of Windsor, with his retreat into self-imposed exile, with the succession of the Queen's father, the question arose as to what was to happen to Balmoral and Sandringham. Windsor had no further use for them and wished to sell them. The Queen's father, who was particularly devoted to Sandringham where he was born, wanted them to remain in the family and agreed to buy them from his brother. Like so much else about royal finances, the price he paid is not known, but it was said at the time to be slightly in excess of £200,000.

However much he paid and whatever he was originally left, the Queen's father, after buying Sandringham and Balmoral, was left with perhaps half a million pounds, or slightly more, in hard cash. Economies during the war years, when there was little or no state entertaining, enabled him to save a further £100,000 from his annual Civil List (at that time £410,000 a year), but at the end of the war he handed these savings back to the Treasury. He was that kind of man. He was also the kind of man who over the last five years of his reign, though the fact did not become public knowledge until after his death, dipped into his Privy Purse (in effect, his salary as monarch) to the tune of £190,000 in order to meet the increasing costs of monarchy and the rising salaries of the Royal Household.

It was because of this that Parliament, when the Queen succeeded to the throne in 1952, approved a Civil List increase of £20,000 so that " about 100 officials of the Royal Household and senior members of the staff who have for several years accepted remuneration lower than appropriate to their duties might have their salaries increased to an appropriate level ". However, this increase to meet royal expenses was largely offset by the Queen's offer to have her Privy Purse allowance reduced by £17,000 a year.

We should perhaps explain that the Civil List—the amount which Parliament grants the Monarch each year—is divided into a number of different sections. That section known as the Privy Purse is, in effect—or was—the Queen's salary, money with which, as in the case of anyone else's salary, she could do as she wished. The difference between it and any ordinary salary was that it was not subject to income tax.

Also included in the Civil List is an amount to pay the salaries of the Royal Household and the Queen's servants and a further amount to meet the expenses of monarchy—food for servants, fodder for horses, petrol for cars and so on. There are other separate allowances for the Duke of Edinburgh, the Queen Mother, Princess Margaret and Princess Anne (Charles has his own income from the Duchy of Cornwall which we will discuss in a moment). There is a further provision to meet the expenses of carrying out public engagements incurred by those Royals not in receipt of an allowance—the Dukes of Kent and Gloucester, Princess Alexandra and Countess Alice of Athlone—but from 1976 (when this was estimated at £120,000) the Queen has met this herself. There is a further small amount for " royal alms and bounty " and the first Civil List of the Queen's reign also included the sum of £70,000 as a hedge against inflation. At the time it seemed reasonable enough. It was to prove hopelessly inadequate.

Just as her father robbed the Peter of his Privy Purse to pay the Paul of Household salaries and expenses, so the Queen, as we have said, volunteered a reduction in her Privy Purse to help meet the increase in the expenses of monarchy. She has since gone a good deal further. In 1971, when the Civil List was increased from its original £475,000 to £980,000 in a belated attempt to catch up with twenty years of inflation, she offered to surrender her Privy Purse altogether. Since then, she has, in effect, been doing the job for nothing, though there is (as we shall see) money from other sources. But all she draws from the state are her expenses. And, these days, not even those in full.

In 1975, when the Civil List was again increased to cope with inflation, this time to £1,400,000 a year, there would have been an even bigger increase if the Queen had not offered to pay £170,000 towards monarchy expenses out of her income from other sources.

Writers like the late Richard Crossman, when they value the Queen's private fortune at £50 million or more, are doubtless confusing the Queen as monarch with the Queen as a private individual. As monarch, she may indeed be worth £50 million or even more if you include the value of the royal art collection, the royal stamp collection, the royal library and all the royal antiques and jewellery which have been handed down from one monarch to the next for generations past.

The royal art collection which includes works by Rubens and Rembrandt, Van Dyck and Canaletto, Titian, Reynolds and Gainsborough as well as several hundred drawings by Leonardo da Vinci, was valued at £15 million as far back as 1958. Today, in the words of Lord Cobbold, its worth must be " astronomical ". The royal antiques take over seventy-five volumes to catalogue. The royal stamp collection, started by George V who devoted three afternoons a week to it, runs to over 330 albums and was valued at more than £1 million over a quarter-of-a-century ago.

The Queen's jewel collection includes more than twenty tiaras and diadems, and goodness only knows how many necklaces, earrings, brooches and bracelets. One tiara, which the Queen refers to as " Granny's tiara " because it was originally made for Queen Mary who gave it to her grand-daughter as a wedding gift, consists of nineteen large drop pearls enclosed by scrolls of diamonds. Another, the Russian fringe or " sunray " tiara, is a graduated circle of solid diamond bars dating from the days of George II which can be worn either on the head or round the throat as a collar. Yet another tiara, once the property of the Grand Duchess Vladimir of Russia, consists of intertwined diamond scrolls in which can be suspended either drop pearls or the magnificent emeralds which have come down from Queen Mary's mother (who won them in a lottery). Other emeralds won in that nineteenth-century lottery have been made into a matching necklace.

While much of the Queen's jewel collection has been inherited, much has also come her way as gifts over the years since birth. She has a necklace of perfectly graduated diamonds with a matching bracelet which were made for her from the twenty-one stones she was given in South Africa on her twenty-first birthday. She has a wattle-shaped brooch of yellow diamonds from Australia; a diamond tiara and matching necklace from the Nizam of Hyderabad; drop pearl ear-rings from the Sheikh of Bahrain; necklace, bracelet and ear-rings in aquamarines and diamonds from Brazil; a necklace of ninety-six rubies from Burma; a fern-shaped diamond brooch from New Zealand. Yet another brooch is made from the huge pink diamond—$56\frac{1}{2}$ carats when mined, 23.6 carats after cutting—which she was given by that "king of diamonds", the late Dr John Williamson.

While the total value of everything—pictures and antiques, stamps, books and jewels—is indeed astronomical, for the Queen to sell any of them, whether gifts or inheritance, would be "unthinkable", as John Colville pointed out during the controversy of 1971. So to assess them as part of the Queen's private fortune is surely as pointless as to judge the contents of the British Museum as belonging to the individual members of the Board of Trustees.

On a more realistic basis, the Queen's inheritance from her father was around half a million pounds. There is no reason to suppose that the financial advice she has had has been any less shrewd than that which Edward VII received in his day and this amount will presumably have grown with the years, probably to something around £2 million, the figure mentioned by John Colville. But this of course, allowing for the dwindling purchasing power of the pound, is no more in real terms than what she inherited in 1952 . . . and probably less.

The expense of upkeeping and maintaining his beloved Sandringham was a consistent drain on her father's purse. It has been less of a drain on hers, thanks to Philip's insistence that the estate there should be less of a sportsman's paradise and more of a viable commercial proposition. But the house itself has still created problems, and in 1974, in an attempt to cut costs, the Queen decided to have it reduced to about three-quarters of its previous size and the remainder modernized. By the following year, when an estimated £100,000 had already been spent on the work, it was realized that, due to inflation, the finished job would come out to at least twice the amount of the original estimate, perhaps more. However reluctantly, the Queen decided that enough was enough and called a halt. She felt, it was explained, that it would be " insensitive and inappropriate " to go ahead at a time " when so many people are facing economic difficulties ".

It was perhaps also " inappropriate " to be seen spending so much of her private money at a time when she was necessarily asking Parliament for yet more money to meet the ever-increasing cost of monarchy.

When the Queen succeeded to the throne in 1952 Parliament approved an annual Civil List of £475,000 with a further £190,000 to be shared between others of the Royal Family. Of this £475,000, the Queen's Privy Purse amounted to £60,000— little more than half the amount her grandfather and great-grandfather drew in their days. The amount allowed for Royal Household salaries and expenses was also less than her grand-father and great-grandfather had had, though £20,000 more than her father was allowed.

These amounts were to remain unchanged for nearly twenty years while inflation at first nibbled and later took big chunks out of them. There were attempts to cut costs. A time and motion study conducted at Buckingham Palace over a nine-month period in 1962/3 produced some small savings. Pages and footmen were told that they would have to make their liveries last for four years instead of three and gardeners had similarly to make their baize working aprons last longer. But these were small drops in the ocean of royal finance . . . and in 1971, to cope with inflation, the Civil List had to be more than doubled to £980,000, a figure more or less in line with the 106 per cent climb in the cost of living since the Queen came to the throne.

Allowances for others of the Royal Family went up at the same time, Philip from £45,000 to £60,000 a year, the Queen Mother from £75,000 to £95,000, Princess Anne from £6,000 to £15,000 (with a further jump to £35,000 when she married Mark Phillips) and Margaret from £15,000 to £35,000.

Despite the fact that the Queen was surrendering her Privy Purse to offset part of the increase, the new figures did not go through Parliament without protest. That arch-opponent of monarchy, Willie Hamilton, said it was " obscene that Parliament should be giving this old lady (the Queen Mother) £95,000 a year " and referred to Princess Margaret as " an expensive kept woman . . . who does rather less than her old mum." Forty-five Members of Parliament voted against the Bill on its second reading, and a public opinion poll showed that while fifty-seven per cent of the public thought the Queen needed some increase, fifty-five per cent considered the amounts too high.

Parliamentary opposition to royal pay packets is nothing new, of course. When Victoria married Albert it was proposed to give him an allowance of £50,000 a year. Parliamentary objections, even in those non-socialist days, saw this cut to £30,000.

The 1971 increase in the Civil List included a further provision against inflation, this time to the tune of £100,000. But with prices now escalating at a rate of twenty per cent a year, with a further jump to thirty per cent soon to follow, it was again to prove completely inadequate. Members of the Royal Household and the Queen's servants, no less than dockers and nurses, car workers, railwaymen and civil servants, needed more money if they were to keep their heads above the rising tide of inflation and in less than four years, like Oliver Twist, the Queen was back asking Parliament for more.

This time there was a right royal row in the House of Commons. The eighty-nine Labour M.P.s who voted against their own Government recommendation to increase the Civil List to £1,400,000, with an annual review from then on, defied a two-line whip to do so. There was no increase in the Privy Purse— in fact, no Privy Purse—and no increase for Philip, Anne, Margaret and the Queen Mum, though there were increases in the expense allowances for Princess Alexandra, her brother, the Duke of Kent, and the new young Duke of Gloucester. These increases, like the other increases in the Civil List, as was stressed time and again in the course of the parliamentary debate, were simply to meet rising costs.

The major part of the 1975 increase in fact—some seventy-five per cent of it—was to meet the Queen's rising wage bill. Nor was this any question of excessively high salaries. The monarchy may perhaps employ too many people—337 full-time and 126 part-time in 1975—but it is not alone in that and it can hardly be said to overpay them. Of all those employed by the Queen at that time, only seven per cent were receiving more than £4,000 a year. The remainder were paid an average of £30 a week, which was certainly not a fortune in 1975 though it was rather more than the Queen paid at the outset of her reign or even in 1971 when the Civil List was previously increased.

A footman joining the palace staff in 1952, the year the Queen succeeded to the throne, was paid £170 a year with annual increments of £5 until he reached a maximum of £190 a year, less than £4 a week. With wages shooting up from £4 to an average £30 a week in twenty years, it was little wonder that the Queen, in 1971, could no longer make the financial ends of monarchy meet. But at least pages and footmen were no longer tempted, as they once were, to augment their slender pay-packets by selling their discarded liveries to travelling circuses and the gold braid from them to back-street jewellers.

Other expenses of monarchy had similarly increased with the years and were to continue to escalate . . . from £291,000 in 1972 to £342,000 in 1973 and an estimated £350,000 in 1974. Between 1972 and 1973 food bills went up from £53,000 to £73,000, the purchase and repair of household goods from £31,000 to £50,000 and even the cost of garden parties from £31,000 to £39,000. Liveries increased from £6,870 to £8,512, laundry from £11,490 to £12,878, horses, forage and farriery from £16,575 to £24,253. There were some savings, but not enough. And further big increases were in prospect for 1975 with fodder for royal horses jumping from £25 to £112 a ton and even the cost of garden parties rising from a mere fifty-seven pence per guest to an estimated £2.

Willie Hamilton was again to the fore in the parliamentary furore which ensued, this time referring to the Royal Family as no more than glorified civil servants, one with " a crown on her head." He was not necessarily against pomp and patronage, it seemed. If that sort of thing attracted " the Yanks and Germans " then it was all right by him. But he wanted " none of the nonsense about them (the Royals) being divinely ordained."

Parliament as a whole did not agree. Nor did many others. When the Queen visited a children's nursery in Bloomsbury, a small boy pressed a tenpence coin into her hand, murmuring that it was " to help with your palace." Momentarily the Queen was taken aback. Then, beaming, she accepted the coin with thanks.

It was an incident echoing the whip-round organized earlier by London dockers when they heard that Philip might have to give up polo for lack of funds. The amount they collected was rather more than tenpence and Philip could hardly accept the money. He asked them to give it to a dockside boys' club instead.

To be fair to Willie Hamilton, the Civil List is not the Queen's only source of income. On the personal side she has the interest from her investments. But these are a private matter and do not concern us here. On the state side, she also has an income from the Duchy of Lancaster, a royal estate dating back to the days of Henry IV. It is made up of urban and rural properties mainly in the Midlands and the North, including the takings from the underground cavern near Peak Castle in Derbyshire, but also includes the rents from the manor of the Savoy in London. In 1973-4 it produced an income of £325,000 and this amount, we are informed, was taken into account when calculating the new Civil List in 1975. In other words, but for the Queen's additional income from the Duchy of Lancaster, the Civil List that year would have been even higher.

For Prince Philip there was no increase in 1975. His money stayed at the £65,000 a year set in 1971. It may sound a lot, but remember that it is not his pay-packet. He has described himself as " self-employed " and, in this sense, he is. His £65,000 a year is the equivalent of the annual turnover in a small business. Out of it he has to pay his own expenses, including the salaries of his aides. But not his overseas travel expenses. These are met either by the Government or whoever has invited him to make that particular trip.

Unlike his wife, however, Philip does pay income tax. The actual amount, of course, as with anyone else's income tax, is a matter of confidence between him and the Inland Revenue, who are doubtless reasonable enough in their assessment of ducal expenses. But on what remains he pays tax at the appropriate levels.

Unlike his father, the Prince of Wales has no income under the Civil List. His money comes from the Duchy of Cornwall, an estate created by Edward III to ensure that his son could live in a style befitting the Black Prince. Curiously enough, the bulk of the estate is not in Cornwall. It consists of farms, villages and apartment blocks, quarries, mines and oyster beds scattered throughout half a dozen different counties, not forgetting the Isles of Scilly. As with the Crown Estates, the most valuable holdings are in London and consist of some forty acres of office and apartment blocks in the vicinity of the Oval cricket ground.

Throughout his minority, under an arrangement agreed between his mother and Parliament, Charles received only a proportion of the Duchy revenues. The bulk of the money—eight-ninths—was handed over to the Treasury to help offset the Civil List. Since celebrating his coming-of-age in November 1969, however, he has been entitled to the entire revenues of the Duchy, valued at £220,000 that year and doubtless more now. Unlike his father, he pays no income tax. Instead, he surrenders a flat fifty per cent of the Duchy income to the Treasury each year. The Duke of Windsor did much the same thing in his days as Prince of Wales, but only to the tune of thirty per cent.

Again in fairness to Willie Hamilton, the cost of monarchy does not end with Civil List payments to the Queen and others of the family. There are considerable additional expenses which have to be met by government departments. There is the cost of maintaining Buckingham Palace, nearly £386,000 in 1972-3. Windsor Castle cost £337,000 that same year and Holyrood-house in Edinburgh another £101,000. By 1973-4 expenditure on royal palaces had jumped to over £1,400,000 with a further £200,000 increase anticipated for 1974-5. The running costs of the royal yacht have climbed to over £1,500,000 a year with the cost of the Queen's Flight creeping steadily towards the £1 million mark.*

Add the lot together—Civil List, other royal salaries, estimated figures for the Duchy of Lancaster and Duchy of Cornwall, royal yacht, Queen's Flight, royal train and all the rest—and the total comes out, give or take a few hundred thousand, at close to £7 million. Which, again giving or taking a few hundred thousand, is about the cost of a General Election or of maintaining the British Embassy in Washington for a twelve-month period.

The Queen, it has been said, is one of the world's highest-paid

* Appendix VI.

monarchs. If you make a straight comparison of the Civil List against the allowances made to monarchs in Belgium, Denmark, Norway, Sweden and the Netherlands, then that is true. But without knowing what extras are involved, comparisons are meaningless.

In any event, in the final analysis it surely boils down to the kind of monarchy you want. As one M.P. said during the course of the 1975 debate on royal finances, " There is no point in having a monarchy if you do not do it in style."

Can Monarchy Survive?

There was a point in Britain's history when it seemed faintly possible that the playboy Prince of Wales who was Queen Victoria's eldest son might not succeed to the throne. He did, and it was perhaps the memory of his own close call which accounted for his gloomy prophecy that his son would be the nation's last monarch.

However, time has proved him wrong. Far from being the last monarch, George V was to win back for the Royals much of the popularity they had lost during the long years of Victoria's widowed seclusion and her son's womanizing. In the words of the late Duke of Windsor, his father " transformed the Crown . . . into a model of the traditional family virtues."

Windsor's own abdication did not exactly help this transformation. But once the first shock-wave had subsided, the clearly happy family life of the brother who succeeded him, that brother's obvious sense of royal duty and courageous struggle against mounting ill-health—these things were to endear him to the nation more than any monarch before him.

His tragic death in 1952 and his daughter's youthful accession saw the Queen come to the throne on a wave of almost hysterical national emotion. She was, in her first few years of monarchy, the subject of almost frenzied adulation which could not and did not last. It had already begun to fade at the time Malcolm Muggeridge and the then Lord Altrincham voiced their strictures of monarchy.

Some of their strictures were not without justification and some still hold good today. Few things about the monarchy have changed over the years since the Queen ascended the throne. There may have been some slight reduction of what might be called " royal ritual "; there has been an increase in the number and variety of people the Royals get to meet; there has been much more royal globe-trotting. Philip, Charles and Anne have all been interviewed on television. But not the Queen herself, though pictures of her in slacks, once regarded almost as *lèse-majesté*, are no longer a novelty. But that is about all. In all else, the monarchy continues to trundle along as traditionally, as anachronistically, as remotely as ever. The Queen, to the majority of her subjects, is still as remote as the moon.

And as with the moon, only a few people are privileged to see her except at a distance. Most see her in close-up only in the newspapers or on television. And just as pictures of the moon give no indication of what lies beneath the surface, nor do those of the Queen. The film *Royal Family* gave a briefly tantalizing glimpse of the woman behind the monarch, but that, at this writing, has been both the beginning and the end. We know many things about her, of course . . . that she is conscientiously dutiful, dotes on her family, is mad about horses and dogs, enjoys crossword puzzles. We do not know what she thinks about women's lib, abortion, trade unions, teenage permissiveness, football violence, and all the other facets of Britain's changed and changing society.

And it could be that the Queen is as remote from those over whom she reigns as they are from her. Largely divorced from the realities, including financial realities, of present-day life, her few contacts with the everyday world abundantly cushioned by those who surround her, it could be for her that life begins and ends almost at the palace railings.

Yet perhaps this is all as it should be—as it must be—in an increasingly uncertain era. Any ideas she herself, her husband or her aides may have had for lessening the remoteness between monarch and people can hardly have been helped by the increasing violence of the age we live in. Leaving aside the attempted kidnapping of Princess Anne as an individual act of a mentally-disturbed man, there have been not a few threats against the Queen and her family in recent years.

There was the threat to blow up the Victoria Tower as she passed beneath it on her way to open Parliament. Following the bomb attack on the Post Office tower, it was a threat to be taken seriously and a huge security operation was set in motion. Similar security, including patrolling helicopters and police marksmen on rooftops, was mounted to protect her when she opened the new London Bridge.

She was threatened by the so-called Angry Brigade prior to a visit to York and there was a threat of assassination—said to come from the I.R.A.—when she toured rural Essex. Whether or not that threat actually came from the I.R.A., that organization has openly stated that it once tried to set up a kidnap plot against the Prince of Wales. And the occasion of his investiture saw not a few bombs exploding in the hills and valleys of Wales.

The Queen, at that time, was seriously concerned for her son's safety. She has shown considerable less concern for her own safety over the years. In 1961 it was suggested that her visit to Ghana, already postponed once because of her pregnancy, should again be called off because of the uncertain situation in that country. She could be in real danger if she went there, she was told.

"Danger," she is said to have replied, "is part of the job."

In 1964, when anti-monarchists battled with the police in the streets of Quebec, when she was greeted with jeers instead of cheers, boos as well as bouquets, one of her entourage suggested that it was not safe for her to drive through the city. "Nonsense," the Queen retorted briskly. "I'll be as safe as houses." She not only drove through Quebec, but was well illuminated by the interior lights of the Cadillac in which she rode. The car was bullet-proof, but it still took courage.

And in 1970, in New Zealand with Charles and Anne, she insisted on going to a concert in Dunedin, despite a threat that bombs would be planted in the royal box. Box, building and the surrounding area were carefully checked first, of course, and the police reported to her that they could find nothing. But think about it for a moment. Would you have gone to a concert in such circumstances? Would you have taken your children? The Queen did.

Whatever her faults of temperament, Anne would seem to have inherited her mother's courage. The only member of the family to have been actually involved in a violent situation, she showed no sign of panic after both her driver and bodyguard had been shot and she herself became the rope in a deadly tug-of-war game between husband Mark and the would-be kidnapper. " I didn't have time to be frightened," she said afterwards.

Like mother, like daughter, like son. Prince Charles was perhaps speaking for the whole family when he said in Melbourne in 1974, " If somebody is going to shoot you, there is nothing you can do about it. Once you start worrying about it, it is time to give up."

Charles has known from early childhood that, the unforeseen apart, the next coronation in Britain will be his. The wait could be a long one, of course. " The Queen is enjoying the very best of health," he told Canadians in the spring of 1975. As a postscript he added that it could be another forty years before he became King.

He was twenty-six at the time. If his own forty-year guess should prove correct, he will be a veteran sixty-six-year-old Prince of Wales when he finally succeeds to the throne, which would make him older than even his great-great-grandfather was when he took over from the nonagenarian Queen Victoria.

There has been some discussion at times as to whether the Queen may one day abdicate in favour of Charles as Queen Wilhelmina of the Netherlands did in favour of her daughter and some astrologers, out to make a name for themselves, have predicted that she will do so. One has even ventured a date, 1978, which is also the twenty-fifth anniversary of her coronation.

Few people, if anyone, took the prediction seriously. The newspapers at least took rather more seriously a throw-away line Philip delivered in the United States. " It has its attractions," he said, grinning, in answer to a question about the possibility that the Queen might abdicate. The furore which followed required an official statement from Buckingham Palace to bring it finally to an end.

" There is absolutely no question of the Queen abdicating," said the palace firmly. That was in 1973.

The same view is held by someone who was sufficiently close to the Queen for a sufficient number of years to have some idea of what makes her tick. " The Queen will never abdicate," this source assures us . . . and the comment made by Prince Charles in Canada would seem to bear out this view.

Whatever the attitude of Willie Hamilton—" none of this nonsense about being divinely ordained "—the Queen, we have

M

reason to believe, regards monarchy as a sacred trust handed down to her by her father, to be held by her as long as her health and strength permit. Prince Philip put it in a nutshell when, in answer to another question concerning possible abdication, he retorted, " Are you asking me when the Queen is going to die?"

Not everyone would agree with this interpretation, of course. And even royal attitudes can change. Certainly some of the folk living around Sandringham have their own reasons for thinking that the Queen will one day abdicate in favour of Charles. They feel she has been " hurt " by some of the things written and said about her recently and is " fed up " to the extent of being quite content to surrender the throne to her son once he has married and settled down. They prophesy that she will retire into private life at her recently acquired farmhouse home near Sandringham. It is perhaps no more than wishful thinking.

For the Queen to abdicate, of course, would be to toss away one of the few remaining values of constitutional monarchy: That it is not at the whim of popular vote, as a presidency is; that it does not chop and change every few years as governments do.

The longer a monarch reigns, the more valuable he or she becomes. Governments and prime ministers come and go. Monarchs, given good health, remain to furnish a link between one government and the next, perhaps even one generation and the next.

It was Disraeli who said, " The longer the reign, the more influence of the Sovereign must proportionately increase. Then it is that the Sovereign can appeal to a similar state of affairs that occurred perhaps thirty years before. A Minister who could venture to treat such influence with indifference would not be a constitutional minister but an arrogant idiot."

One thing is sure. The Queen is not keeping Charles out of things, as Queen Victoria did her eldest son, while Charles, for his part, clearly sees himself playing a separate and individual role as Prince of Wales. Like his father, he appears determined to be no mere royal figurehead.

" I do not intend to waste my years as Prince of Wales," he has said.

The world estate over which the Queen reigns—it can hardly be said any longer that she rules—has shrunk considerably during her term of office and will doubtless continue to shrivel. Grants of self-government to the emergent nations, withdrawal from one-time outposts of Empire and Britain's own dire economic straits, these things have combined to eliminate much of the former grandeur and majesty of monarchy even if the pomp and circumstance is maintained in such ceremonials as the Birthday Parade.

Yet the monarchy in Britain, defying social change at home and political upheaval in the world at large, continues to retain its popularity. It does so by striving to be all things to all people, by sitting tight and saying nothing (or as little as possible) if the going looks particularly rough, of choosing—as Philip said once of royal speeches—to bore people rather than offend them.

Not since Victorian times has there been a real republican movement in Britain and there is little or no evidence of any move towards republicanism today. On the contrary, recent opinion polls have continued to show a three-to-one majority in favour of monarchy and even among the more rebellious younger generation the voting is still two-to-one for. Indeed, even those far-out left wingers who are consistently trying to wreck industry and bring down the Government know better than to try to bring down the monarchy at the same time.

There is, admittedly, a very small, shifting, anti-monarchy lobby which occasionally makes sounds out of all proportion to either its size or importance . . . like the drunken shouts of " Queen out " and " Sieg heil " which greeted her at Stirling university in 1972. But an attempt to repeat the scene, at another university on another occasion, found the police compelled to intervene—to protect the would-be demonstrators!

Britain's royalists, it would seem, can be as quickly hot-headed as any other faction. A socialist councillor who refused to stand for the royal toast during a mayoral lunch at Brighton had his own glass of wine promptly upended over his head.

And not only in Britain. Communist students who gathered to jeer the Queen in New Zealand found themselves being soundly belaboured by sunshade-wielding royalists.

There have been, and will undoubtedly be in the future, demands that the monarchy should cut its coat according to the available cloth. Some people think it is still too rooted in the past and should begin to haul itself firmly into the second half of the twentieth century. But hardly anyone actually wants to see it abolished. And those few who do would be well advised not to try. Any real attempt towards abolishing the monarchy in Britain would be the surest—perhaps the only way—of jolting the vast silent majority out of its recent apathy and inertia.

APPENDIX I

THE QUEEN'S DIARY (1974)

Jan

12 Present church awards to children at Dersingham, Norfolk.

27 Leave London Airport to visit the Cook Islands, New Zealand, Norfolk Island, New Hebrides, the British Solomon Islands, Papua, New Guinea, and Australia. Back 1st March.

Mar

13 Leave for state visit to Indonesia. Back 23rd March.

April

11 Distribute Royal Maundy, Salisbury Cathedral.

21 Take salute at St George's Day parade of Queen's Scouts, Windsor.

30 Welcome the Queen of Denmark and Prince Henrik on their state visit.

May

6 Visit R.A.F. Finningley; Appleby-Frodingham steel works, Scunthorpe.

7 Inspect electrification of British Rail between Preston and Glasgow; attend Scottish Opera gala performance of *The Merry Widow*, King's Theatre, Glasgow.

13 Attend reception given by the Royal Humane Society at Haberdashers' Hall (200th anniversary).

17 Open new Fire Service Technical College at Moreton-in-Marsh.

20 Attend Royal Horticultural Society's Chelsea Show.

21 Give reception for members of the Victoria Cross and George Cross Association.

22 Attend Order of the British Empire service, St Paul's; give reception for officials of Commonwealth countries.

23 Attend reception given by the Administrative Council of King George's Jubilee Trust, Merchant Taylors' Hall.

30 Present colours to the Royal Academy, Sandhurst.

31 Open new Metropolitan Police Training Complex, Hendon.

June

3 Visit Wellington College, Crowthorne.

7 Visit South of England Agricultural Show, Ardingly.

10 Attend garden party for all ranks First Batt., Irish Guards, Caterham.

13 Attend reception given by Royal Society of Arts.

15 Take salute at the Birthday Parade.

17 Attend service for the Order of the Garter, St George's Chapel, Windsor.

July

1 Attend thanksgiving service to mark 1300th anniversary of Hexham Abbey. Visit Newcastle. Take up residence at the Palace of Holyroodhouse.

2 Open new headquarters of the Edinburgh City Police. Visit exhibition at Register House, Edinburgh, to mark bi-centenary. Give garden party at Holyroodhouse.

3 Visit Renfrewshire.

4 Attend service of installation of Knights of the Thistle, St Giles' Cathedral, Edinburgh.

5 Visit Edinburgh Academy (150th anniversary).

9 Welcome the Yang di-Pertuan Agong and the Raja Permaisuri Agong of Malaysia on their state visit.

11 Inspect Yeomen of the Guard.

15 Present new colours to the four battalions of the Parachute Regiment, Aldershot.

16 Give garden party to mark 150th anniversary of the Royal National Life boat Institution.

17 Hold investiture. Attend Royal Tournament, Earl's Court.
18 Give garden party.
22 Attend annual reception of the Imperial Society of Knights Bachelor, St James's Palace.
23 Give garden party.
24 Hold investiture. Attend International Horse Show.
25 Give garden party.
29 Visit Churchill Centenary Exhibition, Somerset House.

Aug
4 Attend memorial service to mark diamond jubilee of the Old Contemptibles, Royal Garrison Church, Aldershot.
7 Embark on H.M.Y. *Britannia* at Southampton.
9 Visit H.M.S. *Neptune* (Clyde submarine base at Faslane). Visit Royal Northern Yacht Club at Rhu.
13 View oil rigs in North Sea, production platform Graythorpe I and visit exploration rig Ocean Kokuei.
14 Visit oil installations at Nigg Bay, Ross and Cromarty.
15 Disembark at Aberdeen and drive to Balmoral.

Oct
17 Visit Commonwealth Institute.
18 Visit Royal Borough of Windsor and Maidenhead.
25 Attend reception to mark fiftieth anniversary of the founding of the Royal Auxiliary Air Force, Guildhall.
29 Open Parliament.
30 Lunch with President and Council of the Royal Albert Hall and inspect redecorations.
31 Dine with the Lord Mayor and Lady Mayoress of London.

Nov
1 Visit Second Batt. Grenadier Guards, Victoria Barracks, Windsor.
6 Open new headquarters of the Royal Academy of Dancing.

9 Attend British Legion Festival of Remembrance, Albert Hall.
10 Lay wreath at Remembrance Day service at Cenotaph.
12 Hold investiture. Visit the Forces Help Society and Lord Roberts Workshops Park Lane fair.
13 Visit Bradford and Halifax.
14 Give reception for delegates to the North Atlantic Assembly.
19 Hold investiture. Visit Queen Elizabeth's College (the Drapers Company's Almshouses at Greenwich) to mark 400th anniversary.
21 Attend première of *Murder On The Orient Express* in aid of the Society of Film and Television Arts.
26 Hold investiture.
27 Visit Royal College of Defence Studies. Give evening reception for members of the Diplomatic Corps.

Dec
3 Hold investiture.
6 Visit I.B.M. plant and Information Services Ltd at Havant. Visit Southampton and open first stage of the Wessex Health Authority's new medical school.
10 Hold investiture.
16 Attend première of *The Island At The Top Of The World* in aid of London Taxi-drivers' Fund for Underprivileged Children.

APPENDIX II

The Succession

The succession to the Throne is governed by the Act of Settlement of 1701. Under this, the Crown passes to the eldest son or to the eldest daughter if there is no son. Should a monarch have no children, the Throne passes to his eldest brother or, if the brother is dead, to his eldest son or, if there is no son, to his eldest daughter. And so on. The present Order of Succession is:

1. The Prince of Wales
2. Prince Andrew
3. Prince Edward
4. Princess Anne
5. Princess Margaret
6. David, Viscount Linley (Princess Margaret's son)
7. Lady Sarah Armstrong-Jones (Princess Margaret's daughter)
8. Richard, Duke of Gloucester
9. Alexander, Earl of Ulster (Duke of Gloucester's son)
10. Edward, Duke of Kent
11. George, Earl of St Andrews (Duke of Kent's son)
12. Lord Nicholas Windsor (Duke of Kent's son)
13. Lady Helen Windsor (Duke of Kent's daughter)
14. Prince Michael of Kent
15. Princess Alexandra
16. James Ogilvy (Princess Alexandra's son)
17. Marina Ogilvy (Princess Alexandra's daughter)

Then come the Earl of Harewood (son of the late Princess Royal) and his sons; his brother, the Hon. Gerald Lascelles and his son; the Duke of Fife (son of the late Princess Maud) and his son and daughter.

APPENDIX III

THE QUEEN'S TRAVELS

As Princess Elizabeth, the Queen visited South Africa, France, Malta, Gibraltar, Greece, Libya, Italy, Canada and the United States, and she was in Kenya (on her way to Australia and New Zealand) at the time of her father's death. Since her Accession she has visited :

1953–4   Bermuda, Jamaica, Fiji, Tonga, New Zealand, Australia, Ceylon, Uganda, Malta, Gibraltar and Libya.

1955   Norway.

1956   Nigeria; Sweden.

1957   Portugal; France; Denmark; Canada and the United States.

1958   Netherlands.

1959   Canada and the United States.

1961   Cyprus, India, Pakistan, Nepal, Iran and Turkey; Italy and the Vatican; Ghana, Liberia, Sierra Leone and Gambia.

1962   Netherlands (semi-private visit to attend the silver wedding celebrations of Queen Juliana and Prince Bernhard).

1963   Australia, New Zealand, Fiji and Canada.

1964   Canada.

1965   Ethiopia, Sudan; West Germany.

1966   Guyana (then British Guiana), Trinidad, Tobago, Grenada, St Vincent, Barbados, St Lucia, Dominica, Montserrat, Antigua, St Kitts-Nevis-Anguilla, British Virgin Islands, Turks and Caicos Islands, Bahamas and Jamaica; Belgium.

1967   Canada; Germany (to review the Royal Tank Regt.); Malta.

1968 Brazil, Chile and Senegal.

1969 Austria; Norway (unofficial visit with Philip and the children).

1970 Fiji, Tonga, New Zealand and Australia; Canada.

1971 Canada; Turkey.

1972 Thailand, Singapore, Malaysia, Brunei, Maldive Islands, Seychelles, Mauritius and Kenya; Yugoslavia; France.

1973 Canada (twice); Australia.

1974 Cook Islands, New Zealand, Norfolk Island, New Hebrides, British Solomon Islands, Papua and New Guinea, and Australia; Indonesia and Singapore; France (a one-day racing visit to see her filly Highclere win the Prix de Diane).

1975 Bermuda, Barbados, the Bahamas and Mexico; Jamaica, Hong Kong and Japan.

APPENDIX IV

PRINCE PHILIP'S TRAVELS

Note: The following are the countries Prince Philip has visited on his own account *in addition* to accompanying the Queen to those countries listed in III.

1952   Finland, Norway and Sweden; France; Malta.

1953   West Germany.*

1954   France and West Germany;* Canada.

1955   Malta; West Germany (twice);* Denmark.

1956   Gibraltar. Seychelles, Ceylon, Papua, New Guinea, Malaya, Australia, New Zealand, Chatham Islands, Deception Islands, South Shetland Islands, Falkland Islands, Tristan da Cunha, St Helena, Ascension Island, Gambia and Gibraltar.

1957   West Germany.*

1958   West Germany (twice);* Belgium; Canada.

1959   India, Pakistan, Singapore, Sarawak, Brunei, North Borneo (now Sabah), Hong Kong, the Solomon Islands, Gilbert and Ellice Islands, Christmas Island, the Bahamas and Bermuda; Ghana.

1960   Malta and Switzerland; West Germany;* Canada and the United States.

1961   West Germany;* Tanganyika.

1962   British Guiana, Venezuela, Colombia, Ecuador, Peru, Bolivia, Chile, Paraguay, Uruguay, Brazil and Argentina; Canada and the United States (twice); Australia, Italy (private); West Germany.*

1963   United States (President Kennedy's funeral);

* These rather frequent visits to West Germany were mainly to visit British forces.

Kenya (private), Zanzibar and Sudan.

1964 Greece (King Paul's funeral); Iceland; Malawi; Greece (wedding of King Constantine and Princess Anne-Marie of Denmark); Malta; Mexico, the Galapagos Islands, Panama, Trinidad and Tobago, Grenada, St Vincent, Barbados, St Lucia, Dominica, St Kitts and Montserrat, Antigua; West Germany,* France and Belgium; Morocco.

1965 Saudi Arabia, Pakistan, India, Singapore, Australia, Sarawak, Brunei, Sabah (formerly North Borneo), Malaya, Thailand, Nepal, Bahrein and Greece; Italy (twice); France (twice); West Germany;* Switzerland; Belgium.

1966 United States and Canada; Netherlands (for the wedding of his nephew, Prince Karl of Hesse); Norway; West Germany (twice);* Jamaica; Argentina; Monaco; Italy; France.

1967 Iran; Australia; France (twice); Netherlands; Italy; Canada (twice).

1968 Australia and New Zealand; Mexico; Ethiopia and Kenya (semi-private); France; West Germany; Canada and the United States; Switzerland.

1970 France; United States; Finland; Italy; West Germany (twice);* Belgium.

1971 Galapagos Islands, Easter Island, Pitcairn Island, Cook Island, Samoa, Fiji, New Hebrides, Solomon Islands, Bougainville, New Guinea and Australia; West Germany (twice);* France; Hungary; Iran; Sweden.

1972 Denmark (King Frederik's funeral); Kenya; Liechtenstein (private); Holland (private); Germany (four times,* one private); Belgium.

1973 Hungary, Yugoslavia, Iran, Afghanistan, India, Thailand, Singapore and Australia; West Germany;* Portugal; Denmark; Soviet Union; Sweden (funeral of King Gustav); Bulgaria; New Zealand and Australia; Belgium; Luxembourg (private).

1974 New Zealand; Australia; France (three times, including memorial service for President Pompidou); West Germany;* Switzerland (twice); Canada and the United States; Germany and Austria (private); Belgium.

1975 Belize, El Salvador, Honduras, Costa Rica and St Lucia; Poland; Morocco.

APPENDIX V

The Queen's Household

Note : Space does not permit us to list all 384 members of the Queen's Household; nor would there be any point to it. But the following are among the more important ones at this writing :

Lord Chamberlain, Lord Maclean.
Lord Steward, Duke of Northumberland.
Master of the Horse, Duke of Beaufort.
Mistress of the Robes, Duchess of Grafton.
Ladies of the Bedchamber, Marchioness of Abergavenny and Countess of Airlie.
Women of the Bedchamber, Hon. Mary Morrison, Mrs John Dugdale, Lady Susan Hussey, Lady Abel Smith.
Extra Women of the Bedchamber, Hon. Mrs Andrew Elphinstone and Lady Rose Baring.
Private Secretary and Keeper of the Queen's Archives, Lt-Col. the Rt Hon. Sir Martin Charteris.
Deputy Private Secretary, P. B. C. Moore.
Assistant Private Secretary, W. F. P. Heseltine.
Assistant Keeper of the Queen's Archives, R. C. Mackworth-Young.
Press Secretary, Ronald Allison.
Assistant Press Secretaries, Mrs Michael Wall and R. E. Moore.
Keeper of the Privy Purse and Treasurer, Major Sir Rennie Maudsley.
Assistant Keeper of the P.P., Major S. G. B. Blewitt.
Deputy Treasurer, R. D. Wood.
Comptroller (Lord Chamberlain's office), Lt-Col. Sir Eric Penn.
Assistant Comptroller, Lt-Col. J. F. D. Johnstone.

Master of the Household, Vice Admiral Sir Peter Ash-
more.
Assistants to the M.O.H., Michael Timms, R. Winship.
Crown Equerry, Lt-Col. Sir John Miller.
Palace Steward, J. Walton.
Chief Housekeeper, Miss Victoria Martin.

APPENDIX VI

The Cost

In addition to the amounts paid to the Queen and other members of the Royal Family under the Civil List, the following expenses of monarchy are borne by various government departments.

	Actual 1973–4 £s	Estimated* 1974–5 £s
Upkeep of palaces and royal residences	1,423,916	1,602,000
Royal Yacht	1,653,738	1,509,700
The Queen's Flight	895,000	971,000
Royal Train	47,537	201,100
Overseas visits requested by government departments	302,238	175,440
Office machinery and stationery	104,806	102,000
Marshal of the Diplomatic Corps	5,853	6,000
Gentlemen at Arms and Yeomen of the Guard	14,692	16,000
Central Chancery of the Orders of Knighthood	20,638	29,000
Equerries	24,713	30,850
Totals	£4,493,131	£4,643,090

* Supply Estimates, March 1974.

N

APPENDIX VII

Year of Accession		Date of Death	Age at Death	Length of Reign
1553	Jane (Lady Jane Grey)	1554	17 (beheaded)	9 days
1553	Mary Tudor	1558	43	5 years
1558	Elizabeth I	1603	69	44 years
1689	Mary Stuart (joint-sovereign with husband William)	1694	33	6 years
1702	Anne	1714	49	12 years
1837	Victoria	1901	81	63 years
1952	Elizabeth II			

Index

Index

A

Abel Smith, Lady, 191
Abergavenny, Marchioness of, 191
Adeane, Lord, 20, 157
Airlie, Countess of, 191
Albert, Prince Consort, 119, 146, 149, 150, 151, 169
Albert Victor, Prince, 38
Albrecht, Prince, 15
Alexander of Tunis, Earl, 91
Alexandra, Princess, 14, 82, 165, 169, 185
Alexandra, Queen, 37
Alice, Princess, Countess of Athlone, 165
Alice, Princess, Duchess of Gloucester, 14
Alice, Princess, of Battenberg—see ANDREW, PRINCESS
Allison, Ronald, 158, 191
Altrincham, Lord, 76, 78, 131, 174
Amies, Hardy, 106
Amin, Idi, 93-4
Andrew, Prince, 13, 30, 38, 79, 81, 86-7, 95, 97, 103, 185
Andrew, Princess, of Greece, 13, 87
Anne, Princess
    birth, 13
    character, 87-8, 123
    childhood, 73, 81-2
    courtship, 88, 90
    education, 82
    finance, 165, 168, 169
    kidnap attempt, 91-2, 176-7
    marriage, 90-1, 92-3
    riding, 88
    royal duties, 87
    other, 19, 30, 38, 58, 80, 125, 130, 175, 176, 185
Anne, Queen, 148-9, 194
Anne-Marie, Queen of Greece, 89, 189
Annigoni, 117
Argyll, Duke of, 76
Armstrong-Jones, Antony—see SNOWDON, EARL OF
Armstrong-Jones, Lady Sarah, 14, 83, 185
Ascot, Royal, 20, 148-9
Ashmore, Vice Admiral Sir Peter, 158, 192
Attlee, Clement, 56
Auriol, Vincent, 56
Award Scheme, Duke of Edinburgh's, 115-16
Ayckbourn, Alan, 29

B

Bahrain, Sheikh of, 167
Balmoral, 20, 28, 40, 48, 53, 80, 148, 149-51, 157, 162, 164

Baring, Lady Rose, 191
Beaton, Inspector James, 92
Beatrix, Princess, 15
Beatrix, Princess of the Netherlands, 89
Beaufort, Duchess of, 50
Beaufort, Duke of, 50, 191
Bernhardt, Prince of the Netherlands, 72, 186
Birendra, King of Nepal, 137
Birkhall, 40, 42, 48
Birthday Parade, 20, 32, 34, 38-9
Blair, General Sir Chandos, 94
Blewitt, Major S. G. B., 191
Brabourne, seventh Baron, 15, 78
Brabourne, Lady—*see* MOUNT-BATTEN, LADY PATRICIA
Britannia—*see* ROYAL YACHT
Browning, Lieut. General Sir Frederick, 55
Buccleuch, Duke of, 42
Buckingham, Duke of, 143
Buckingham Palace, 18, 25, 28, 29-30, 31, 45, 53, 63, 77, 141-8, 153, 172

C

Callaghan, James, 93, 94, 96
Callender, Alex, 92
Cambridge, Lady Mary, 52
Carl Gustaf, King of Sweden, 95
Cassell, Sir Ernest, 164
Catto, Lord, 29
Chan, Jackie, 80
Chaplin, Sir Charles, 36
Charles, Prince—*see* WALES, PRINCE OF
Charteris, Lieut. Colonel Sir Martin, 55, 59, 156-7, 191
Childs, Stanley, 129
Christina, Princess, 15

Churchill, Sir Winston, 61, 63, 66, 74, 83, 157
Clarence House, 18, 19, 55, 61, 63, 74
Clarissa, Princess, 15
Cobbold, Lord, 161
Colour, Trooping the—*see* BIRTHDAY PARADE
Colville, John, 162, 167
Colville, Sir Richard, 158
Connaught, Duke of, 129
Constantine, King of Greece, 89, 189
Cornwall, Duchy of, 163, 165, 171-2
Crawford, Marion, 39, 40, 50
Crossman, Richard, 166
Crown Estates, The, 163

D

Dean, John, 60
De Gaulle, Charles, 80
Denness, Mike, 29
Devonshire, Duke of, 42
Dionne quins, 56
Disraeli, Benjamin, 178
Dolan, Ken, 26-7
Dorothea, Princess, 15
Dugdale, Mrs John, 191

E

Edinburgh, Duke of
    appearance, 114
    Award Scheme, 115-16
    birth, 13
    character, 114, 117-18, 119-20, 121, 124-6
    father, as, 73, 90, 116-17, 129, 131

finances, 165, 168, 169, 171
flying, 120-1, 135
speeches, 85, 123-4, 125, 127-8
sport, 118
travel, 56-7, 58, 75, 79, 99, 100, 104-5, 109, 111, 121, 123, 188-90
work, 30, 65, 117, 121-2
other, 19, 26, 29, 33, 34, 48, 54, 55, 60, 62, 64, 68, 74, 78-9, 89, 136, 140, 141, 146-7, 148, 150, 151, 175, 177
Edward VII, King, 37, 45, 141, 151, 164, 174
Edward VIII, King—*see* WINDSOR, DUKE OF
Edward, Prince, 13, 20, 30, 38, 83, 185
Elizabeth, Queen, the Queen Mother, 13, 23, 26, 29, 33, 37, 43, 44, 45, 48, 49, 50, 52, 58, 61, 62, 68, 71, 84, 85, 86, 91, 94-5, 101, 116, 130, 131, 165, 168, 169
Elizabeth II, Queen
accession, 13, 17, 58-62, 174
appearance, 21
A.T.S., in, 34, 52
birth, 13, 37
character, 18-19, 21-5, 40-1, 49, 52, 54
childhood, 36-43
corgis, 27, 29, 41, 147
coronation, 13, 66-70
education, 41, 47
fashions, 41, 53, 54, 106-8
finances, 161-73
health, 65, 78
horses and racing, 40, 54, 72, 148-9
jewels, 24-5, 41, 166-7
leisure, 30-1, 53, 80-1

marriage, 13, 55
mother, as, 72-3, 129, 135, 136, 176
photography, 110-11
royal duties (as Princess Elizabeth), 51-2, 53-4, 55
silver wedding, 23, 88-9, 138
training for monarchy, 18, 38-9, 46-8
travels, 32, 54, 56-7, 72, 76, 77, 78, 85, 91, 97-113, 186-7
work, 18-21, 25-35, 62-3, 64-5, 72, 76-7, 82, 181-4
Elphinstone, Mrs Andrew, 191
Ethiopia, Emperor of, 72

F

Fairchild, John, 108
Feisal, King, 72
Fermoy, late Lord, 58
Fife, Duke of, 185
Fox, Jeremy, 29
Frederik, King of Denmark, 82, 189
Frederika, Princess, 15
Frederika, Queen of Greece, 83
Funfrock, Huguette, 93

G

George III, King, 143, 163
George IV, King, 143, 148
George V, King, 14, 37, 42, 45, 61, 69, 164, 166, 174
George VI, King, 13, 17, 18, 37, 43, 44-6, 47, 48, 50, 55, 57, 58, 64, 103, 136, 141, 157, 164, 174
George, Prince of Hanover, 15

George, Prince of Hohenlohe-Langenburg, 15
Gibbs, Sir Humphrey, 85
Glamis, 40, 42
Gloucester, Duchess of, 14, 90, 92
Gloucester, Duke of, 14, 89, 90, 92, 165, 169, 185
Gloucester, lake Duke of, 14, 37, 42, 62, 90, 92, 164
Gloucester, Prince William of, 14, 89-90
Gloucester, Princess Alice, Duchess of, 42, 64
Gordon, Sir Robert, 149
Gorton, John, 19
Grace of Monaco, Princess, 89
Grafton, Duchess of, 191
Graham, Lieut. General Howard, 108
Grey, Beryl, 29
Guelf, Prince, 15
Gustav, King of Sweden, 189

H

Hahn, Dr Kurt, 126
Hamilton, William, 76, 93, 94, 117, 169, 170, 171, 172, 177
Hampshire, Susan, 139
Hardinge, Sir Alexander, 157
Harewood, Earl of, 14, 40, 185
Harewood, late Earl of, 14
Hartnell, Norman, 54, 65
Hawkins, Anne—see WALL, MRS MICHAEL
Henrik, Prince of the Netherlands, 181
Heseltine, William, 158, 191
Hicks, Ashley, 16
Hicks, David, 15
Hicks, Mrs David—see MOUNTBATTEN, LADY PAMELA

Hicks, Edwina, 16
Hicks, India, 16
Hills, Denis, 93
Hills, P.c. Michael, 92
Hirohito, Emperor of Japan, 100
Hirsch, Baron Maurice de, 164
Holt, Harold, 134
Holyroodhouse, Palace of, 31, 148, 172
Hussein, King, 72
Hussey, Lady Susan, 191
Hyderabad, Nizam of, 167

I

Investitures, 20, 31
Iran, Shah of, 72

J

Jenkins, Roy, 96
Johnstone, Lieut. Colonel J. F. D., 192
Jolson, Al, 36
Jones, Tom, 127
Juliana, Queen of the Netherlands, 186

K

Karl, Prince of Hesse, 15, 189
Kennedy, John F., 81, 188
Kent, Duchess of, 14, 80, 116
Kent, Duke of, 14, 80, 165, 169, 185
Kent, late Duke of, 14, 37, 42, 164
Kent, Prince Michael of, 14, 89, 185
Knatchbull, Amanda, 15
Knatchbull, Joanna, 15

Knatchbull, Michael, 15
Knatchbull, Nicholas, 16
Knatchbull, Norton, 15
Knatchbull, Philip, 16
Knatchbull, Timothy, 16
Kraft, Prince, 15

L

Ladies-in-waiting, 154, 191
Lancaster, Duchy of, 163, 171
Langtry, Lillie, 151
Lascelles, Sir Alan, 157
Lascelles, Hon. Gerald, 14, 40,
    185
Lascelles, Henry, 15
Lascelles, James, 15
Lascelles, Mark, 15
Lascelles, Robert, 15
Lascelles, Viscount, 15
Lebrun, Albert, 46
Lightbody, Helen, 131
Liles, Margaret, 138
Linley, Viscount, 14, 185
Lloyd George, David, 134
Lord Chamberlain, The, 154-6,
    191
Loss, Joe, 96
Lowe, Arthur, 29
Ludwig, Prince, 15
Luncheon parties, 29-30, 75

M

Macdonald, James, 58, 62
Macdonald, Margaret ('Bobo'),
    40, 60, 64, 113
Mackworth-Young, R. C., 191
Maclean, Lord, 191
Macmillan, Harold, 24

Malaysia, King of, 32, 182
Margaret, Princess
    birth, 13, 38
    finance, 165, 168, 169
    marriage, 79-80
    romance, 71-2, 74
    separation, 96
    other, 40, 41, 46-7, 48, 50,
        52-3, 58, 62, 82, 185
Margrethe, Queen of Denmark,
    32, 181
Margarita, Princess of Baden, 15
Margarita, Princess of Hohen-
    lohe-Langenburg, 15, 84
Marina, Princess, 14, 42, 64, 84,
    87
Marten, Sir Henry, 48
Mary, Princess Royal, 14, 84,
    185
Mary, Queen, 14, 18, 26, 37,
    38-9, 41, 42, 43, 44, 47, 50,
    51, 53, 61, 65, 66, 141, 142,
    147, 166, 167
Maud, Princess, 185
Maudsley, Major Sir Rennie,
    191
Maundy, The Royal, 20, 32, 34,
    63
Maximillian, Prince, 15
McConnell, Brian, 92
Menzies, John, 24
Michael, Prince—*see* KENT,
    PRINCE MICHAEL OF
Miller, Lieut. Colonel Sir John,
    192
Moore, P. B. C., 191
Moore, R. E., 191
Morrison, Hon. Mary, 191
Mountbatten of Burma, Earl, 15,
    120, 136
Mountbatten, Lady Pamela, 15
Mountbatten, Lady Patricia, 15
Muggeridge, Malcolm, 76, 125,
    174

N

Nevill, Lord Rupert and Lady, 81
Norfolk, late Duke of, 61
Northumberland, Duke of, 191

O

Ogilvy, Hon. Angus, 14, 82
Ogilvy, James, 15, 83, 185
Ogilvy, Marina, 15, 185
Oliver, Alison, 88
Oxley, Tom, 138

P

Parker, Commander Michael, 55, 59, 60, 75
Paul, King of Greece, 83, 189
Peebles, Katharine, 73
Penn, Lieut. Colonel Sir Eric, 191
Philip, Prince—*see* EDINBURGH, DUKE OF
Phillips, Captain Mark, 13, 88, 90-1, 92, 168, 176-7
Plunket, late Lord, 72
Pompidou, Georges and Mme, 111, 189
Prior-Palmer, Lucinda, 88
Privy Council, 20, 27-8, 31

Q

Queen's Flight, The, 104, 172, 193
Queen's Household, The, 153-9, 165, 169, 191-2

R

Rainier, Prince of Monaco, 89
Rainier, Prince (Philip's nephew), 15
Richards, Sir Gordon, 72
Roberts, Granville, 59
Rooney, Mickey, 93
Roosevelt, Franklin D., 47
Ross, Sir Alexander, 29
Royal Family (film), 23, 86, 158, 175
Royal Lodge, Windsor, 40, 41, 48, 80
Royal warrants, 156
Royal yacht, 72, 75, 104-5, 172, 193
Ruprecht, Prince, 15
Russell, Ronald, 92, 146

S

St Andrews, Earl of, 14, 185
Salote, Queen of Tonga, 68-9
Sanders, David, 29
Sandringham, 20, 28, 38, 58, 61, 65, 80, 90, 148, 151-2, 162, 164, 178
Scoles, R. F. and J., 156
Simpson, Mrs—*see* WINDSOR, DUCHESS OF
Smith, Ian, 85
Snowdon, Earl of, 13, 79-80, 96
Sophie, Princess, 15, 84
Steiger, Rod, 93
Strathmore and Kinghorne, fourteenth Earl, 37
Streisand, Barbra, 102

T

Theodora, Princess, 15, 84, 87

Thomas, Ian, 106
Timms, Michael, 192
Townsend, Peter, 53, 71-2, 74, 96
Trudeau, Pierre, 29
Truman, Harry S., 57, 71

U

Ulster, Earl of, 14, 92, 185

V

Valentino, Rudolph, 36
Victoria, Queen, 45, 47, 65, 94, 143, 146, 149, 150, 151, 163, 169, 174, 178, 194
Volterra, Mme, 72

W

Wales, Prince of
    acting, 82
    birth, 13, 129
    character, 138-9
    childhood, 73, 130-31
    created Prince of Wales, 79
    education, 49, 78, 82, 131-3, 133-4
    finances, 165, 171-2
    flying, 88, 135-6
    humour, 138-9
    investiture, 87, 134-5
    naval career, 136-7
    romance, 31, 137-8
    royal duties, 132, 134-5
    travel, 137
    other, 24, 26, 29, 30, 46, 58, 68, 89, 175, 176, 177, 185
Wall, Mrs Michael, 191
Walton, J., 192
Warfield, Mrs Wallis—*see* WINDSOR, DUCHESS OF
Watts, Maurice, 18-19
Wellesley, Lady Jane, 31, 138
Wellington, Duke of, 31, 138
William III, King, 162
William IV, King, 143
William, Prince—see GLOUCESTER, PRINCE WILLIAM OF
Wilhelmina, Queen, 177
Williamson, Dr John, 167
Wilson, Sir Harold, 93
Windsor Castle, 20, 28, 29, 48-9, 77, 80, 82, 148-9, 172
Windsor, Duchess of, 14, 43, 64, 77, 80, 84, 86, 89, 157
Windsor, Duke of, 14, 18, 26, 37, 38, 40, 42-3, 44, 64, 80, 84, 86, 89, 156, 157, 164, 172, 174
Windsor, Lady Helen, 14, 83, 185
Windsor, Lord Nicholas, 14, 185
Winship, R., 192
Wood, R. D., 191

Y

York, Duke of—*see* GEORGE VI, KING